Architects' Designs for Furniture

Published in association with
The Royal Institute of British Architects
Drawings Collection

Jill Lever

Architects' designs
for furniture

NEW YORK

For Jonathan, with love

Published in the United States of America in 1982 by
Rizzoli International Publications, Inc.,
712 Fifth Avenue,
New York, NY 10019

First published in Great Britain by
Trefoil Books Ltd, 1982

The publishers wish to acknowledge the generous
support of the Headley Trust in the preparation
and production of this book.

ISBN 0 8478 0442 9 (hardback)
ISBN 0 8478 0443 7 (paperback)

Set by Elephant Productions, London
Printed and bound by Eyre and Spottiswoode Ltd
at the Thanet Press

Contents

Preface

The Royal Institute of British Architects is very proud to be the custodian of its incomparable British Architectural Library, of which the Drawings Collection forms an important part. In scope the Collection is the largest and most comprehensive body of architectural designs in the world, with a quarter of a million drawings from the Renaissance to the present day. It is naturally orientated towards British drawings, great numbers of them presented by the architects themselves, but it contains also some magnificent Continental groups, notably the Drummond Stewart collection of Baroque theatre designs and the Burlington Devonshire collection which includes almost all the surviving drawings of Palladio, perhaps the most influential architect in history.

The Collection is exhaustively organised, but the use made of it by the whole international community imposes very considerable pressures on the RIBA, for published catalogues are of necessity costly. I was delighted, therefore, when the Headley Trust asked us to find a way to produce a number of illustrated books to make the treasures of the Collection known to a wider public, and to follow this by travelling exhibitions on some of the themes selected.

The fruit of this enlightened patronage is the present series of substantially illustrated books, each supported by a scholarly text, on widely different aspects of the Collection. I am confident that they will give as much pleasure to others as they have given to me.

Owen Luder
President, Royal Institute of British Architects

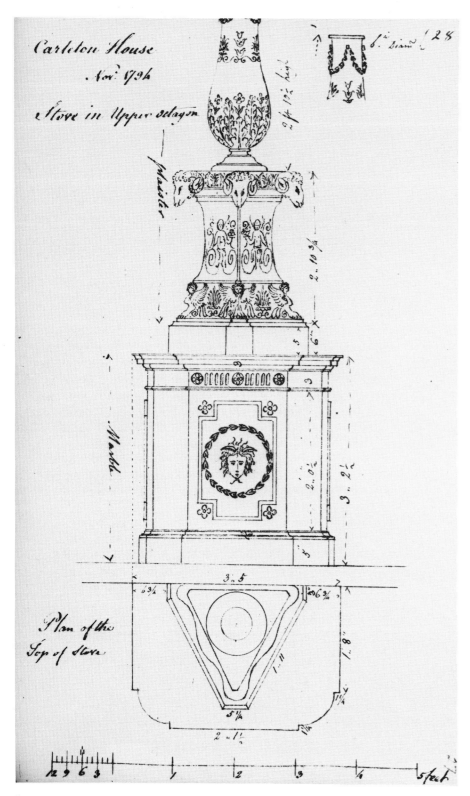

Carleton House
Nov: 1794

Stove in Upper Octagon

Plan of the
Top of Stove

Foreword and acknowledgements

A dusty day sorting an architect's drawings is often enlivened by the discovery, among the rolls and sacks and large tin trunks of designs and working drawings for buildings, of, say, a vivid design for wallpaper or a saucy one for a fountain. Before the useful, or decorative, arts became each the province of specialist designers, architects were often (and still are sometimes) involved in the design of textiles, wallpapers, metalwork, stained glass, ceramics, graphics, costume, stage scenery, gardens and, of furniture. The purpose of this book is to invite attention to some of the architects' designs for furniture in the Drawings Collection of the Royal Institute of British Architects and to suggest what has been the architect's special contribution in this field. 'Furniture' usually defined as 'the movable contents of a house or room' has been stretched to include William Kent's royal barge (furniture-like in its design), garden furniture, some built-in furniture and the furniture and decoration of entire rooms.

There are important collections of architects' drawings for furniture in other museums. In particular, those of Robert Adam in the Sir John Soane Museum, London, C.R. Mackintosh's drawings at the University of Glasgow and designs from a number of architects at the Victoria and Albert Museum, London. While this cannot be a comprehensive survey, it is hoped that it will be a useful contribution to a subject that Charles Handley-Read (1918-1971) was the first to investigate. His books and notes (now in the RIBA Library and Manuscripts Collection) have been of the greatest help. I am especially grateful to Mr Clive Wainwright of the Victoria and Albert Museum for his kindly advice and to Miss Hilary Grainger, Mrs Karen Moon, Miss Jan Murton, Miss Selden Wallace and Miss Sally Williams who have shared with me the results of their respective researches on Sir Ernest George, George Walton, Marcel Breuer, Alfred Waterhouse and Sir Edwin Lutyens. I should also like warmly to thank for their help, Mrs Jill

Allibone, Mr Nicholas Antram, Professor J.H.G. Archer, Mr Geoffrey de Bellaigue, Mr John Brandon-Jones, Miss Nancy Briggs, Mrs Mosette Brodrick, Mr J. Burchell, Mr Geremy Butler (who took the photographs), Mr R.C. Buxton, Mr S. Cantacuzino, Lady Cobham, Mr D.E. Coult, Dr J. Mordaunt Crook, Mr B.R. Curle, Mr David Dean, the Earl of Derby, Miss Angela Doughty, Dr Penelope Eames, Mr R.E. Enthoven, Mr P.R. Field, Mr D.V. Fowkes, Mr Max Fry, Mr Ernö Goldfinger, Mr Ian Grant, Mr W.T. Halford, Dr Eileen Harris, Mr John Harris, Mr Robin Hartley, Mr Richard Horden, Mr Simon Jervis, Sir Cyril Kleinwort, Lord Lambton, Mr Jeremy Lever, the Hon. Mrs M. Lubbock, Mrs Angela Mace, Dr Michael McCarthy, Miss Sally MacDonald, Mr Mervyn Miller, Sir Geoffrey Newman, Mr John Outram, Mrs David Peake, Miss Jane Preger, Mr Robert Price, Mrs Margaret Richardson, Mr Godfrey Ruben, Mr Nicholas Savage, Mr M. Urwick Smith, Mrs Alison Smithson, Lord Stanley of Alderley, Mr Gordon Stobbs, Mr Peter Thornton, Dr Julian Treheurz, Mr J.F.V. Vandeleur-Hoover, Miss Lavinia Wellicome and Mr Gerald Yorke.

Jill Lever
June 1982

List of Colour Plates

Roman numerals refer to the plates, arabic numerals to the pages where they are reproduced: a detailed caption will be found with the material on each architect.

The front cover shows John Vardy's design for a daybed (plate I) and the back of the cover Ernö Goldfinger's design for a living room (page 128).

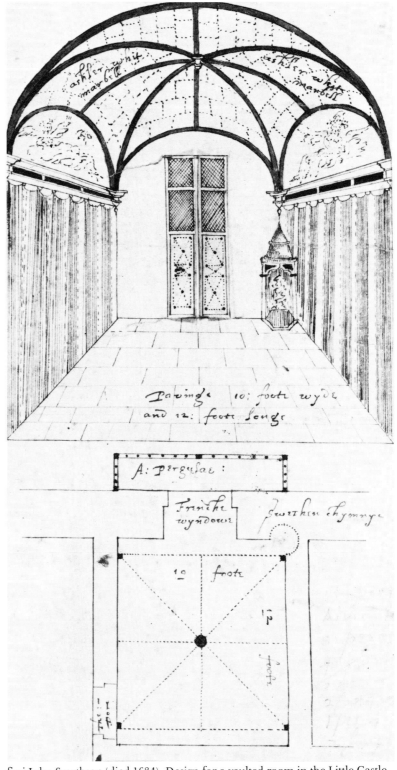

ashler whit marbell

ashler whit marbell

Pavinge 10: foote wyde
and 12: foote longe

A: pergula:

Frinche wyndowe

pwithin chymnye

10 foote

12

foote

fig i John Smythson (died 1634). Design for a vaulted room in the Little Castle, Bolsover Castle, Derbyshire, c.1625.

Introduction

The design of furniture is not and never has been the sole prerogative of any one profession. Furniture-makers, artists, engineers, talented amateurs and others have all designed furniture, for it is only recently that furniture design has become the subject of formal training. Since architects seldom sign their furniture, the evidence for their involvement relies on documents and up to the 18th century, drawings, account ledgers, bills and published sources are very sparse. Thus the medieval architect's contribution to domestic furniture design rests largely on the wealth of architectural detail — blind arcading, colonnettes, blank tracery, crenellations and the like — on surviving chests, cupboards and benches. The earliest surviving medieval furniture designs are those for a lectern and stall in Villard de Honnecourt's 13th century sketchbook, now in the Bibliothèque Nationale, Paris.

The earliest, known, surviving design for English domestic furniture is that by John Smythson (died 1634) for a bed (fig. 2). It was drawn about 1600 as was the design for a closet (fig. 1) by John's father, Robert Smythson (1534/5-1614). Taken with their other designs for such useful things as a device for training horses, brewing equipment and a frame saw (in the Smythson collection at the RIBA), they demonstrate the versatility and ingenuity of mason-trained architects. John Smythson's design for a room with a balcony at Bolsover Castle (he worked there from 1611 to 1634) with its marble vaulted ceiling, painted decorations, corner chimneypiece, shuttered *French Windowe* and wall hangings under a cornice indicates that architect's concern with the unity of a room (fig. i).

However, the idea of a building with architecturally integrated interiors in the modern sense began to emerge, in England, with Inigo Jones (1573-1652). Alas, none of his designs for furniture have survived though he must surely have made some, for, as Peter Thornton wrote in *Seventeenth-Century Interior Decoration in England, France & Holland* (1978), 'one suspects that Inigo Jones, back in the 1620s and 1630s, cannot have been content to have his neatly ordered schemes ruined by the introduction of the ordinary run of clumsy Jacobean furniture'. And Jones's designs for chimneypieces, overmantels, ceilings and wall treatment serve to indicate the kind of detailed attention that interiors might receive from an exceptional architect. Jones's pupil and architectural heir, John Webb (1611-72) left only a single design for furniture and that was for the state bed shown in his elevation of the alcove in the King's Bedchamber at Greenwich Palace (fig. 3). Dated 1665, Webb's design shows a French influence, in particular that of Jean Le Pautre, a leading French architect whose engraved designs were available in England from about 1660. Even more influential in this country was Daniel Marot, a Hugenot architect and designer, known both from his published designs and for the work he did for King William III at Hampton Court and at Kensington Palace.

It was the court of Louis XIV that set the pace in matters of household style and taste. And it was in France that royal architects first assumed a dictatorial control over every aspect of interior design. In Restoration England, the Stuart court and its circle employed French upholsterers, French or Dutch carvers and cabinet-makers and French and Dutch furniture was brought across the Channel. French influence is reflected in the design, made about 1699, by William Talman (1650-1719) for a Thames-side villa, its gardens, internal decoration and furniture (fig. 4). But a design (in the Victoria and Albert Museum, London) of possibly the same date, by William's much-travelled son John (1677-1726) for a room for a collector is a good deal more eclectic in its sources (fig. ii). Opulent and even bizarre, it is the first known English example of a design that fully integrates furniture, decoration and architecture. An alternative wall elevation has tall, narrow bookshelves set into walls that flank arched recesses housing the chimneypiece and a glazed bookcase. Mouldings of similar profile are on picture frames and cabinets while scallop shells and luxuriant foliage unite walls, ceilings and furniture. In this use of the recurring motif, Talman exploited one of the architect's fundamental contributions to furniture and interior design, a contribution only possible when the role of the architect as the one controlling mind was accepted by the patron. Since the elevations reveal an intimate knowledge of the objects that were to be placed in the room and since Talman was an inveterate collector — 'the most unwearied conservator of all that could be called curious' — it seems likely that he designed the room for himself. And it is tempting to suppose that it may have

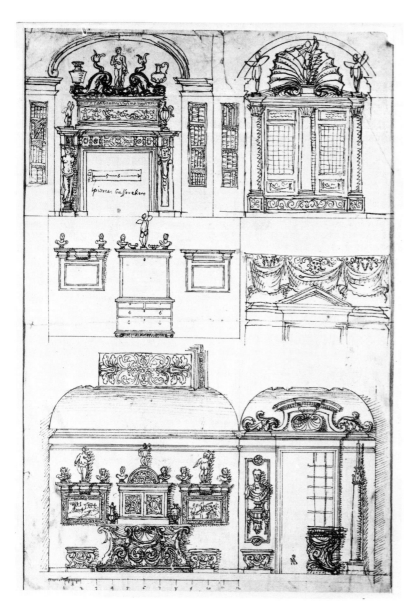

fig ii John Talman (1677-1726). Alternative designs for a room, before 1726. *(Victoria and Albert Museum, Department of Prints and Drawings)*

It seems unlikely that the Talmans were the only architects of the late 17th century to have designed, at least, some furniture. Whether, say, Sir Christopher Wren, Sir Roger Pratt, Hugh May, William Winde or Sir William Bruce designed any is a matter for speculation. Through travel on the Continent they would certainly have been aware of the trend towards unified interiors but it was not until the 18th century that the architect as designer fully emerged.

Though the contribution made by James Gibbs (1682-1754) to furniture is slight, his designs of the 1720s and '30s for mirrors, console tables and clocks using motifs taken from Baroque, Rococo and Palladian sources suggest an interest in that field. It was a contemporary, William Kent (1685-1748) who must be counted as the first significant documented English architect-designer. While the exteriors of his buildings were composed in a soberly correct Palladian style, his designs for internal decorations were wonderfully sumptuous. Since neither Palladio nor Inigo Jones had left any direct precedents for furniture design, Kent used approved motifs taken from their architecture and also from Antique animal forms to evolve strongly three-dimensional, carved and richly gilded pieces. John Vardy (died 1765) published in 1744 *Some Designs of Inigo Jones and William Kent* and thus made the Kentian manner more accessible (fig. iii). Vardy's own designs were strongly influenced by Kent (fig. 6) as were, for example, those of Henry Flitcroft (1697-1769). But Kent's influence was most felt in the designs for bookcases, presses and cabinets which, framed between pilasters or columns, crowned by cornice or entablature and pediment, lent themselves, along with mirrors, particularly well to architectural treatment.

This kind of architectural furniture, derived by Kent from Inigo Jones's designs for doorways and chimneypieces, was not universally popular. Batty Langley (1696-1751) who published designs for Tuscan, Doric and Ionic bookcases[1] wrote that 'when a Gentleman applies himself, with a good design for a Bookcase, &c made by an able Architect . . . most of the Masters in this Trade [that is, the cabinet-makers] they instantly condemn it; and alledge 'tis not possible to make Cabinet Works look well, that are proportioned by the Rules of Architecture'.[2] The complaint that architects mis-applied architectural or masonry details to timber finishings and furniture is an old one. It was probably levelled against furniture designed by medieval architects. For as Alphonse Warrington wrote of Norman Shaw's Gothic cabinet of 1861[3]: 'in woodwork, architecture is a mistake: architects designing furniture too often forget this, as did their brethren of the thirteenth and sixteenth centuries . . . when they were only architects and not upholsterers'. 'Dolls' houses', 'toy architecture' and 'wooden buildings masquerading as furniture' are only some of the criticisms of architect's furniture. Of course, to the purist, details designed to deal with external conditions when brought indoors *are* illogical. Sir William Chambers wrote that 'some . . . object to pediments in interior decorations; because, say they, where the whole is covered and

been intended for the villa at Thames Ditton that both Talmans prepared designs for at this time. In any case it emphasises the fact that the most comprehensive schemes are often those made by the architect for himself.

W. Kent inv.   I. Vardy delin et Sculp.

fig. iii William Kent (1685-1748). Design for a table, plate 41, *Some Designs of Mr Inigo Jones and Mr William Kent*, published by John Vardy, 1744.

enclosed, there can be no occasion for coverings to shelter each particular part' and then countered this by arguing that 'beauty and fitness, are qualities that . . . in architecture . . . are sometimes incompatible'.[4] And Chambers's design for a bookcase (fig. 11) with its cornice, pilasters, arched doors and architectural ornament is untroubled by ideas about fitness for purpose.

William Jones (died 1757) though a minor architect had the distinction of publishing in 1736 (as an appendix to James Smith's *Specimens of Antient Carpentry*) some of the earliest designs for furniture to

appear in England. Of the side-tables and pier-glasses that were illustrated, a few were in a Rococo style while others reflected both Kent's vigorous sculptural manner and his more architectural style. Batty Langley, who built very little but published a great deal, introduced in his *Ancient Architecture Restored . . .* (1741-2) the Gothic style for domestic interiors. To Palladian, Rococo and Gothic was added, by the 1750s, the Chinese style which was given a sort of respectability by Chambers's publication of *Designs of Chinese Buildings, Furniture, Dresses etc.* in 1757. Other architect-designers known through

fig iv Robert Adam (1728-1792). Designs for furniture for Kenwood House, Hampstead, London, plate viii, *The Works in Architecture of Robert and James Adam I*, published 1773-8.

Plate I: see page 42

Plate II: see page 44

the engraved designs of pattern books include William Halfpenny, Timothy Lightoler and (later) John Crunden and John Carter. The first pattern book entirely devoted to furniture was cabinet-maker Thomas Chippendale's *Gentleman and Cabinet-Maker's Director* (1754) in which the designs were mostly in the Rococo style particuarly associated with his name. Later, Chippendale was to publish designs in a Neo-Classical style whose introduction was due to three architects: William Chambers, James Stuart and Robert Adam.

Sir William Chambers (1723-96) seems to have been responsible for the first strictly Neo-Classical piece of furniture actually made in England — the President's chair of the Royal Society of Arts, 1759. But the designs done about 1757 for interiors and furniture for Kedleston Hall by James Stuart (1713-88) appear to be the earliest surviving designs in that style and though they were not executed the drawings were there when Robert Adam took over from Stuart and clearly formed the basis for some of his earliest furniture designs.

While Chambers and Stuart were, for different reasons, only occasional designers of furniture, Robert Adam (1728-92) designed more furniture than any other 18th century architect (fig. iv). In his interiors he wrought 'a kind of revolution . . . an almost total change . . . in the decoration of the inside'. Though the notion that Adam designed everything within within a building including carpets that echo the designs of the ceilings above them, plate, chandeliers, door furniture and so on, is attractive, on the basis of his surviving drawings in the Soane Museum, London it is true of only two or three of his commissions. He designed a quantity of seat furniture, but his most characteristic contributions are those pieces that, allied to door and window cases, chimneypieces, alcoves, niches, pilasters, friezes and panels, completed his wall compositions. Such pieces — mirrors, side-tables and commodes (often with flanking pedestals and urns) as well as bookcases, organs and cabinets — were specifically designed for a particular location. Proportions, details, decorative motifs and finish were intimately related to the surroundings and a great deal is lost when Adam's furniture is divorced from the interiors for which it was designed.

By the mid-1770s, as the number of competitors increased, Adam's dominance in the field of furniture design declined. Among architects, George Richardson, Thomas Leverton and James Wyatt all designed in a Neo-Classical manner derived from Adam, Wyatt moving on to a greater individuality in which ornament became sparser and rectilinearity yielded to more flowing forms. Joseph Bonomi (1739-1808) had worked in the Adam office but his designs were more severely masculine than those of Adam (figs. 17 & 18). William Porden (*c.* 1755-1822) designed in a Neo-Classical style (figs. 15 & 16) and, as at Eaton Hall, 1804-12, in a Gothic style, both influenced by the work of James Wyatt (1746-1813) to whom he had been apprenticed. Sir John Soane (1753-1837) whose few furniture designs (in the Soane Museum) are as Peter Ward-Jackson wrote in his *English Furniture Designs of the*

Eighteenth Century (1959) 'good enough to make us regret that not more have survived' was almost certainly the author of the tables and chairs designed for the library at Stowe in about 1805, in a Gothic Perpendicular style of great individuality.

Just as the first phase of Neo-Classicism in furniture had been pioneered by architects, the second phase, late Neo-Classicism, more often, though imprecisely, called the Regency style, was also initiated by architect-designers. The dominant style from the 1790s until the early 1840s, it had its beginnings in Henry Holland's (1745-1806) work of the 1780s and some of his designs were first brought to the attention of the public through *The Cabinet-Maker and Upholsterer's Drawing-Book* published in four parts between 1791 and 1794 by Thomas Sheraton, drawing master, publisher and, possibly, furniture designer too. A reaction against the over-refinement of Adam's later work, Holland's designs (figs. 19 & 20) were influenced by contemporary French sources and from 1794 by the drawings of Antique decoration and furniture made by C.H. Tatham (1772-1842) who had been sent by Holland to Italy for that purpose. Those drawings were published in 1799-1800 as *Etchings of Ancient Ornamental Architecture drawn from the Originals in Rome and other Parts of Italy during the years 1794, 1795 and 1797* and provided archaeologically correct exemplars that were widely used by furniture-makers, metalworkers and other craftsmen.

The archaeological tendency in Regency furniture was reinforced by the publication in 1807 of another important source book — *Household Furniture and Interior Decoration* by Thomas Hope (1769-1831). Hope, an amateur architect and connoisseur, based his designs on close observation of Antique prototypes taken from, for example, the painted decoration of Greek vases of which he owned a great many (fig. v). However his designs were too uncompromisingly archaeological, and uncomfortable as well, for the general taste and it was through the vulgarized versions published in cabinet-maker George Smith's pattern books that Hope's Greek and Egyptian designs were most widely known.

J.B. Papworth (1775-1847) designed furniture not only as part of his architectural schemes but also for furniture firms. Nor was he the first architect to do so for Vardy, for example, in the 18th century had a family interest, through a brother, in a firm and so, later, did C.H. Tatham. In the 19th century it was to become more and more common for architects to design for furniture firms and in some cases, having completed their architectural training, to devote themselves entirely to the design of furniture. Papworth was something of an all-rounder both in his activities and in his range of styles. But his most characteristic productions in architecture and design are essentially in the Classical style of the Regency period. In furniture, Papworth allowed his admiration of the French Empire style some scope but generally his work was described as in the 'Grecian or modern style'. The term comes from J.C. Loudon's *Encyclopaedia of Cottage, Farm and Villa Architecture and Furniture* published in 1833 and it was thought at

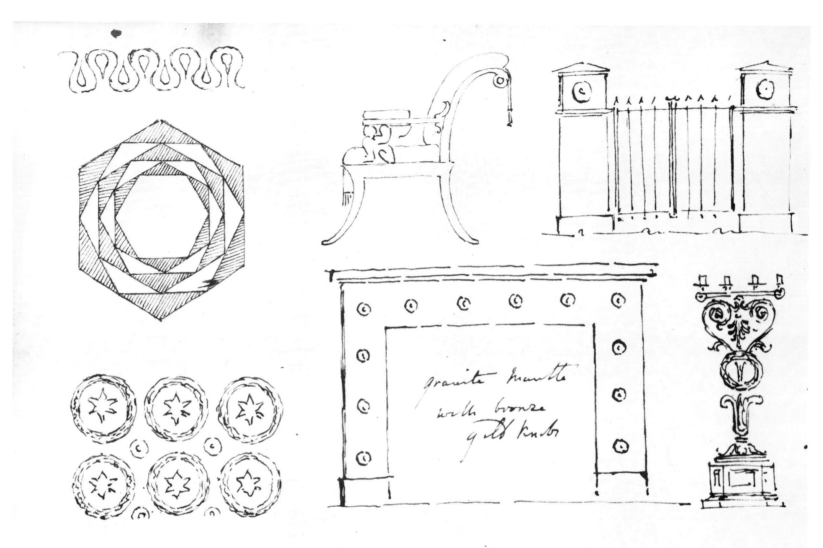

fig v Thomas Hope (1769-1831). Designs for a klismos chair, candelabrum, gate, mantel and ornamental details, c.1812, page 42 from a sketchbook.

the time that the examples of 'Grecian or modern' were heavily plagiarized versions of Papworth's designs. The vast *Encyclopaedia*, unlike most previous architectural publications, was not intended for the aristocracy or those catering for it but was addressed to the interests of the middle classes, whose increasing numbers provided a growing market for the furniture-maker as well as the builder. Thus the book provides not only a useful reminder of an important change in the nature of patronage but also a very convenient list of the principal styles in furniture at the time. Loudon named these as 'the Grecian or modern style, which is by far the most prevalent; the Gothic or perpendicular style, which imitates the lines and angles of the Tudor Gothic architecture; the Elizabethan style, which combines the Gothic with the Roman or Italian manner; and the style of the age of Louis XIV, or the florid Italian, which is characterised by curved lines and excess of curvilinear ornaments'.[5] For designs in the Gothic and Elizabethan styles, Loudon relied on his assistant Edward Buckton Lamb (1806-69), providing the young man 'with abundant opportunities for indulging a copious, unruly and undiscriminating imagination'.[6] Lamb's design (at the RIBA) for a monogrammed chair for himself in his favourite Tudor style is, with its throne-like form, engagingly self-important (fig. vi).

Of the four styles named by Loudon, Louis XIV or florid Italian (a revival of French 18th century taste) was used in the 1820s by Lewis Wyatt (1777-1853) and his cousin, B.D. Wyatt (1775-c.1855) and by Philip Hardwick (1792-1870) in 1834, for carved and gilded furniture for town and country houses and London clubs. As Baroque-ish Louis Quatorze slid into Rococo-ish Louis Quinze, its use by architects, which was never considerable, declined. Though C.J. Richardson (1806-71) used it in the 1850s for a cabinet (fig. 45) sketchily designed in a manner that merged with the so-called Naturalistic style in which convoluted plant forms replaced the curves and scrolls of Rococo.

Sir Jeffry Wyatville's (1766-1840) first use of the Elizabethan style for furniture dates from about 1815. An octagonal table, designed in 1823 for Ashridge Park (fig. 27) uses spirally turned legs that were not in fact introduced until the last half of the 17th century. However, Elizabethan was a freely interpreted style that incorporated Jacobean and Stuart features without embarrassment. Anthony Salvin (1799-1881), the best known architect and designer in the Elizabethan style and an authority on the architecture and decoration of the period, used a free version for the furniture he designed for Mamhead (fig. 18). The publication by an architect, T.F. Hunt, of *Exemplars of Tudor Architecture adapted to Modern Habitations with . . . Observations on the Furniture of the Tudor Period* in 1830 and of *Specimens of Ancient Furniture* in 1836 by another architect, Henry Shaw, offered illustrations of genuine pieces and gave further stimulus to the English antiquarian styles that were employed, with greater or lesser degrees of popularity, for another century.

The Gothic style from its introduction for furniture in the mid-18th century tended towards a papery application of Medieval details to current forms. Thus B.D. Wyatt's hall bench of 1814 (fig. 25) has contemporary tapered legs and curved sides with acanthus enrichment, wedded to crocketing and blind tracery. The design by Wyatville for an octagonal porters' table (fig. 26) made in 1823 borrows its form from a 15th century octagonal font and is an ingenious attempt to reach a Gothic solution. A.C. Pugin's *Gothic Furniture* (1827, first published in *Ackerman's Repository of Arts*, 1825-7) offered interesting but inexact examples of designs for furniture in a Gothic style.

Gothic became a vehicle for reform in 19th century design only when the carefree mining of its decorative possibilities yielded to an understanding of its grammar. The connexions between the style, structure and function of Gothic architecture were established by A.W.N. Pugin (1812-52) in *True Principles . . .* (1841) and other books. His earliest designs were for furniture that, archaeologically incorrect, he later deplored as youthful enormities and burlesques (figs. 36 & 37). But *Gothic Furniture of the Fifteenth Century* (1835) has some designs that while immature were correct and too, used revealed construction. It was the use of 'honest' or revealed construction and of solid (not veneered) wood allied to strongly emphasised structural bracing that marked Pugin's mature designs for furniture (fig. 40). Pugin's rationalising influence, derived from the principles of 'convenience, construction and propriety' that he formulated for his buildings, was felt into this century but seems to have been only slowly absorbed by contemporary designers. William Butterfield (1814-1900) and G.E. Street (1824-81) designed furniture that showed his influence, while Sir Gilbert Scott (1811-1878) in his design for a table for Kelham Hall (fig. 46) did not.

fig vi Edward Buckton Lamb (1806-1869). Design for a chair for the architect's own use, *c.*1835, page 72 from an album.

21

Pugin was the first of the Victorian reformers of the applied arts. His revolt against the irrationality, shoddiness and vulgarity of commercial furniture was taken up by a second generation of progressive designers who were either practising architects or who had, as in the case of William Morris (1834-96) received an architectural training. Throughout the 1850s and early 1860s, Gothic Revival continued to be the style of reform though the model was now the muscular, pointed Gothic of the 13th century rather than the flattish Perpendicular that Pugin had used. A characteristic of much architect-designed furniture of the period was its massive scale and eye-catching architectural detail, and decoration. Painted decoration was introduced from about 1856 by William Burges (1827-81) who designed it in a thoroughly whole-hearted manner in which figurative painted panels were combined with abstract motifs that served to emphasise the lines of cabinets, bookcases, wash-hand-stands and the like (figs. 47 & 48).

Bruce Talbert's (1838-81) massy designs, influenced no doubt by Burges and by J.P. Seddon (1827-1906) were published in *Gothic Forms Applied to Furniture* in 1867-8. Another non-practising architect, C.L. Eastlake (1836-1906) published *Hints on Household Taste* in 1868 and the down-to-earth character of his ideas — plain, cheap to make and moderately scaled-made them suitable for ordinary homes and they were particularly influential in America.

From about the mid-1860s, progressive designers began to move away from Gothic Revival forms and motifs to a less rigidly historicist approach. R. Norman Shaw (1831-1912) whose first exercise in furniture design, in 1861, was in the agressive manner of Burges, moved on within a year or two to invent (with W.E. Nesfield, 1835-88) the Old English style. Based upon vernacular sources, its appeal lay in its flexibility and simple and additive vocabulary (fig. 58). It was probably through Shaw that Alfred Waterhouse (1830-1905) was introduced to the style. Unlike Shaw, Waterhouse used it only once for his architecture but after some initial experiments in a Puginian Gothic retained it for his furniture until the late 1880s (figs. 59 to 61).

The Old English style bridged the gap between the Gothic Revival and the 'Art Furniture' of the Aesthetic Movement that flourished most strongly in the 1870s. E.W. Godwin (1835-86) was certainly the most original of these designers. The light and elegant pieces that he designed for Dromore Castle in 1869 (figs. 54 to 57) show Japanese and other influences but Godwin's real importance lies in an originality remarkably free, for his time, from historicism.

Art furniture continued in popularity throughout the 1870s though an alternative style, 'Queen Anne', was employed by some architect-designers. 'Queen Anne' was not, as its name might suggest, a straight revival of the style of the early 18th century but rather a free treatment of 17th and 18th century sources. The progenitors of the style include Philip Webb and the Morris circle, Shaw and Nestfield, G.F. Bodley (1827-1907) and George Gilbert Scott Jnr (1839-97). Scott designed furniture for his clients, for himself (fig. 32a) and for a firm that he set up with Bodley and Thomas Garner (1839-1906) in 1874 called Watts & Co. (figs. 32b,c). Scott used 'Queen Anne' with discretion, choosing features mostly from 17th century (and especially, Carolean) sources. Particularly associated with the 'Queen Anne' style is Maurice B. Adams who published designs in the journal, *Building News* and in 1888 brought out *Examples of Old English Houses and Furniture with Some Modern Works from Designs by the Author*. Ernest Newton (1856-1922) was for his first years in practice a 'Queen Anne-ite'. His sideboard of 1884 (fig. 72) is in that manner though so exuberant that it verges on Free Renaissance, another contemporary historicist style.

The Renaissance style had made occasional appearances since the 1840s and the sofa, designed in 1840 for the Reform Club, by Sir Charles Barry (1795-1860) has a faint suggestion of Renaissance detail to its basically Regency form (fig. 34). More assured Renaissance motifs appear on Sydney Smirke's (1799-1877) handsome bookcase for Luton Hoo designed in 1849 (fig. 23) and more elaborate and accomplished still is George Aitchison's (1825-1910) sideboard, designed in 1874 (fig. 62). By the 1880s Free Renaissance based on English, French, Italian, Dutch, German and Spanish Renaissance sources was used by a number of architects including R.W. Edis (1839-1927) and T.E. Collcutt (1840-1924) for both their buildings and their furniture. Ernest George (1839-1922) used mainly Jacobean sources for Poles, a house that he designed in 1890-2 and the drawing room was furnished with pieces based on late 16th and 17th century examples (fig. 71). George was an avid collector of furniture and objects and his work as a furniture designer demonstrates the influence of collecting upon design. Other architects collected too but while in the case of, say, Pugin this led to an understanding of the principles that lay behind design, for George it led only to skilful adaptations of existing prototypes and did nothing to further the design of furniture. By the 1880s, reform lay in the hands of the designers of the Arts and Crafts Movement, impelled by the revulsion against the debased standards of Victorian commercial design experienced by Pugin and the Gothic Revivalists.

The design philosophy and practice of the Arts and Crafts Movement was rooted in the work of Pugin, Morris, Ruskin and Philip Webb (1831-1915). Webb (like William Morris) had trained in the office of G.E. Street and there he learned the use of revealed construction, solid wood and strongly emphasised joints that Street had admired in Pugin's furniture. Much of Webb's design work was done for Morris's firm that, quite soon after it was established in 1861, used vernacular as a design source. Webb's design for a sideboard of about 1870 (fig. 63) was influenced by country-made furniture of the 17th century and in the Webb/Morris circle, the forms and details of farmhouse and cottage furniture were appreciated both for the style of life that produced them and for their honest, straightforward construction. Webb's influence continued into the 1890s and is apparent in the work of two of his disciples: W.R. Lethaby (1857-1931) and George Jack

Plate III: see page 46

Plate IV: see page 49

Design for a Sideboard

5 feet

Plate V: see page 55

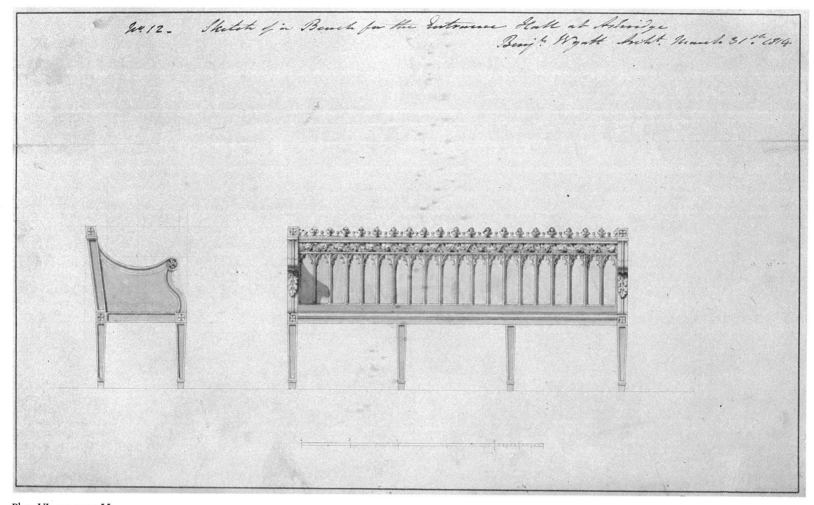

Plate VI: see page 55

(1855-1932) both of whom were architects and who also designed for the Morris firm.

Inspired by a romantic socialism and believing that reform was best accomplished in association, many Arts and Crafts practitioners set up guilds and exhibition societies. The first of these was the Century Guild founded in 1882 by the architect A.H. Mackmurdo (1851-1942) and Selwyn Image (1849-1940), a designer and illustrator. It was soon followed by others including the Guild of Handicraft, established in 1888 by C.R. Ashbee (1863-1942) an architect whose best work in the applied arts was some ravishingly beautiful metalwork. In 1890, five architects: Reginald Blomfield (1856-1942), W.R. Lethaby, Mervyn Macartney (1853-1932), Ernest Gimson (1864-1919) and Sidney Barnsley (1865-1926) each put £100 into a firm they called Kenton & Co. When it folded up two years later, while three of them cut their losses, Gimson and Barnsley decided to set up a workshop in Gloucestershire and so began the Cotswold school of furniture that was to have a continuing influence throughout the first half of the 20th century.

Probably the best known of the Arts and Crafts designers is C.F.A. Voysey (1857-1941) who like Pugin, Burges, Godwin and Webb designed for a wide range of the decorative arts. The simplicity and elegance of his furniture was, as in the case of his architecture, highly influential (figs. 73 to 77). George Walton (1867-1933) who, as with Pugin and Eileen Gray (1879-1976) came to architecture after first having designed furniture, designed some pieces that reflect Voysey's manner (fig. 79) though unlike Voysey he readily accepted 'historical echoes' from a variety of sources (fig. 80). M.H. Baillie Scott (1865-1945) designed distinctive box-ey furniture decorated with pretty Art Nouveau-ish flowers. His interest in unified interiors with recesses, galleries, inglenooks, screens and built-in furniture was shared by Barry Parker (1867-1947) (fig. 88) and his bold use of colour and geometrical motifs by Edgar Wood (1860-1935) (figs. 86 & 87).

The last of the 19th century designers was Charles Rennie Mackintosh (1862-1928) and far more than any of his contemporaries his reputation has been an international one. Today, his highly-prized furniture is available in facsimile versions made by an Italian firm that also replicates furniture by Rietveld and Le Corbusier. Like many (perhaps most) architects, Mackintosh began by designing furniture (from about 1890) for his own use. All of his important pieces were done as part of the programme for his buildings and interiors (fig. vii).

Mackintosh's work and that of his Arts and Crafts contemporaries continued into the first years of the 20th century but no other pioneering individual or group emerged to take over the baton that had passed from Pugin to successive reformist movements in the relay race of 19th century design. British designers lost the lead and Mackintosh's achievement can be seen as so far unequalled in the 20th century.

The years around 1900 were distinguished in architecture and in design by an almost obsessive cult of individuality, a bewildering variety of revived styles, free styles and an occasional near-style-lessness. J.Henry Sellers (1861-1954) a Manchester architect whose work is associated with the Arts and Crafts Movement, turned like some of its members to models from the 18th and early 19th centuries and produced some urbane and highly finished furniture. Halsey Ricardo (1854-1920), an Arts and Crafts eclectic, seems to have used Regency models for chairs that accompanied a desk (fig. 85) both ornamented with semi-Art Nouveau motifs. Giles Gilbert Scott (1880-1960) based his designs for furniture and decoration, of about 1915, on Pompeiian sources studied at first hand (figs. 102 & 103). Earlier, in 1905, E.A. Rickards (1872-1920), a leading Edwardian Baroque architect, used French Rococco for a sideboard designed with his typical panache (fig. 101).

The master of several styles, Sir Edwin Lutyens (1869-1944) set up in practice at the early age of twenty, designing furniture almost from the start and in a vernacular-derived Arts and Crafts manner. Within a few years he acquired an appreciation of joiner-made 17th century furniture and Stuart models that together with Mary and William ones became a constant source for his furniture designs. It was perhaps the broad effect, generous proportions and geometry that appealed to him. From about 1907 Lutyens sometimes introduced more or less direct copies of antique furniture into his schemes and did so for Viceroy's House, New Delhi (1912-31) (figs. 92 to 95) where he also designed furniture with Indian-derived details (fig. 98) and other pieces that were pure exercises in geometry. Lutyens's furniture from the 1930s has sometimes been confused with that designed by his son, Robert (1901-1972) who in 1927 went into partnership with R.W. Symonds (1889-1958) an architect, designer and furniture historian. The furniture they designed was either Neo-Georgian, Regency or 'modern' geometrical in character and examples of their work were included in the architect J.C. Roger's *Modern English Furniture* published in 1930 by Country Life. With few exceptions the furniture illustrated is either by the conservative Cotswold school of Gimson, the Barnsleys and designer-craftsmen Gordon Russell (1892-1980) and Peter van der Wals (1870-1937) or else tasteful historicist examples by Sir Edwin Lutyens (in a William and Mary style), J. Henry Sellers and Sir Robert Lorimer (1864-1929). 'Swedish Modernism' was represented by Edward Maufe (1883-1974) from (fig. 104) and colourism by Robert Atkinson (1883-1952). Modernity was left to the Russian-born Serge Chermayeff (born 1900) who married into the conservative furniture firm of Waring and Gillow in 1928 and immediately began designing for them furniture that was by turn Art Deco, 'Jazz Modern' and 'Moderne'. But he soon moved into a fully committed Modernism.

An important concern of the furniture designers of the Modern Movement was with the possibilities of new materials and inventions: chrome-plated tubular steel, preformed plywood, laminated wood,

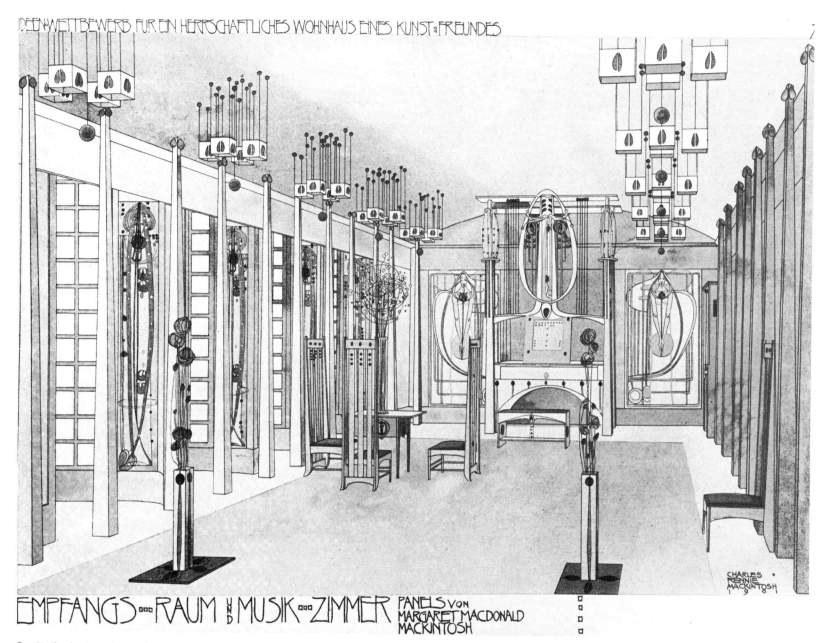

fig vii Charles Rennie Mackintosh (1862-1928). Design for a music room, plate
7, *Haus eines Kunstfreundes*, Darmstadt, 1902.

aluminium, latex foam, tension springs and with old materials used in new ways. Wells Coates (1895-1958) designed plywood furniture from the early 1930s for a newly created furniture firm called Isokon. And when Marcel Breuer (1902-81) came to Britain in 1935 he designed for that firm the Long Chair, the only generally accepted classic piece of pre-war modern furniture design produced in Britain.

In 1936, Heal & Son Ltd put on an exhibition of architect-designed furniture called *Seven Architects*. The exhibitors were E. Maxwell Fry (*b.* 1899), Christopher Nicholson (1905-48), Jack Howe (*b.*1911), Chrisopher Heal (*b.* 1911), Brian O'Rorke (1901-1974), Raymond McGrath (1903-1977) and Marcel Breuer. The aim of the exhibition was to stimulate better standards of design for, as a survey of 'The Design of Furniture in Britain' commissioned by *The Studio* and published in 1937[7] revealed, the majority of furniture was of inferior quality, tasteless, banal and often descended to 'depths of horror which defy description'. Generally, the state of furniture design in Britain was described as moribund and 'nearly every impetus that has come into the furniture trade for better design has come from outside, and from architects'. A less favourably disposed critic, though, sourly described the intervention of architects as 'the ultra-modernists play[ing] about with industrially produced materials and claim[ing] a lot of attention'.[8]

While architects of the 1930s continued to design one-off, experimental pieces for their schemes (figs. 109-113, 128-129) many were also designing for production. These included, as well as Chermayeff, Wells Coates (fig. 132) and Breuer, others like Ernö Goldfinger (*b.* 1902) (fig. 114), McGrath (fig. 127), Oliver Bernard (1881-1939), O'Rorke and Misha Black (*b.* 1910).

In 1939 war brought a halt to most building or design work not concerned with the national effort. From November 1942 only Utility furniture (designed in an 'evolved modern Gimson style' thought retrograde by some) was manufactured and continued in production until the early 1950s. During the war years, critics such as Herbert Read had argued the need for replacing the existing system of design education based on craft practices with a technology-oriented approach. His suggestion that the Royal College of Art should become a university of design for industry was implemented in part when from 1951 the College introduced its diploma of design. The 1950s marked the decline of 'the universal acceptance of architecture as the analogy for design' and with it 'the architect's claim to be absolute master of the visual environment'.[9] An independent design profession became established in which training was based on anthropometrics (man and measurements), ergonomics (relationship between man and equipment) and on the new technology created by plastics. From now on 'furniture is made for man . . . and not to *go with* the room for which it is designed'.[10]

For the architect 'creative choice' from a wide range of internationally designed and manufactured furniture has almost replaced one-off design. However, the furniture and other objects selected will often have been designed by architects. The undoubted classics of the 20th century design have come from the drawing boards of architects or architectually trained designers like Breuer, Mart Stam, Mies van der Rohe, Le Corbusier (with Charlotte Perriand), Alvar Aalto, Charles Eames, Bertoia, Saarinen, Magistretti, Arne Jacobsen, Tobia Scapa and others. Alison and Peter Smithson's (1928- & 1923-) 1964 change-of-address note with its eclectic gaggle of Thonet, Rietveld, Breuer, Mies, Bertoia, Jacobsen and Eames-designed chairs together with their own prototype pogo chair, saddle chair and egg chair (designed for the *House of the Future* exhibition, 1956) illustrates one example of such choice (fig. viii).

Foster Associates house project of 1979 was furnished with an equally international assortment of furniture that includes Hans Coray's perforated aluminium chairs designed in 1938 and other furniture designed by Italian, Finnish and German designers between 1969 and 1978 together with the architects' own design for a swivel-armed stereo-television-lights system (fig. ix).

Post-Modernism has produced furniture that expresses that movement's pre-occupation with metaphor and language. John Outram's (*b.* 1934) designs for His and Her chairs, designed with other furniture for a country house abroad, translates the 'syntax of the building into the medium of the furniture'[11] (fig. x). Which is to say that the chairs' vertical members have a correspondence with the piers to the house that, made of stripped grey concrete, crushed brick concrete, white marble and yellow brick are themselves expressions of a sedimentary accumulation. In the building, the capitals to the columns are spheres within a cube and this form is reflected in the knee-joints of the chair. The segmentally arched chair rail has an equivalence in the form of the roof and in an arched chimneypiece. The curtains were perhaps suggested by the proscenium-like appearance of the chair back and thus the seat becomes the auditorium. The translation of building forms into furniture has many precedents and most notably, in this century, in the work of Frank Lloyd Wright.

That architects choose to design for the applied arts is due to a number of reasons, the most fundamental of which is that what they require is not available. New styles of architecture create new kinds of interior spaces that have to be matched by new finishings and furniture. The products of conservatively-minded workshops or of commercial manufacturers have not always commended themselves to the innovatory or fastidious architect who may then decide to design his own furniture. Another stimulus lies in the desire to control all aspects of a scheme. The opportunities for total design rely not only on the ability of the architect to design comprehensively but also upon his client's acquiescence. In the 18th century, for instance, the social life and pleasures of the aristrocracy depended a great deal upon the exercise of 'Taste'. And many patrons were reluctant to forego the

fig viii Alison and Peter Smithson (1928- & 1923-). Change-of-address note, 1961.

pleasures of a direct involvement with the craftsmen they employed or of personal visits to the showrooms-cum-workshops of chair-makers, joiners, cabinet-makers, carvers, gilders, clock makers, lamp makers, stuccateers, wallpaper printers, carpet makers, embroiderers, upholsterers and other craftsmen who in London gathered in and around St Martin's Lane. Even those architects particularly associated with the concept of total design such as Adam, Pugin, Voysey or Mackintosh achieved it in only a few of their commissions. It is not surprising therefore that many of the best examples of comprehensive design occur in houses designed by the architect for himself. Here, even the smallest items — keys, inkstands, toastracks — might well be designed by the architect owner.

The first major example of unified design in a public building was the New Palace of Westminster. A recent inventory of furniture in the House of Lords has revealed the astonishing range and quantity that Pugin designed between about 1844 until his death in 1852. In all, at least 1,156 pieces of 325 different types have survived and, of arm chairs alone, there are forty-nine distinct types.[12] A survey now being made of Waterhouse's furniture for Manchester Town Hall indicates that at least fifty and perhaps as many as a hundred types of furniture exist still. In both cases, a great many pieces have survived and that is unusual. The rate of obsolescence between a building and its contents differs and it is this lack of unchanged interiors complete with furniture, together with the patchy survival of documents that makes it difficult to establish the extent to which buildings were comprehensively designed in the past. This also makes it very important that where such interiors survive intact that they should remain so.

'Thematic unity', 'total harmony', 'the linking motif', which is to say, the integration of building, interior and contents, can only be achieved by an architect. When volume, form and detail are sensitively integrated or cunningly contrasted, the aesthetic pleasures are intense. When eye and mind discover, for instance, that curved walls are matched by architraves and doors of the same curvature and that the geometry of walls, doors, ceiling and floor in an oval room are accentuated by ornament executed in a variety of media, and that tables and chairs reflect the form and details of the room then some basic human need for order and wholeness is satisfied. And the sheer cleverness and audacity are appealing too.

The design of furniture can offer an opportunity for experiment since it is both cheaper and quicker to furnish than to build. New ideas related to style or stylelessness may emerge sooner in a design for a cabinet than for a house. The cool clarity of Greek detail that James Stuart derived from his archaeological research in Greece was first used as the basis for his designs for furniture and interior decoration. Godwin realized an almost abstract rectangularity in his furniture ten years before his designs for 44 Tite Street, made in 1878. And the search for new structural ideas may be achieved first in an architect's

Plate VII: see page 64

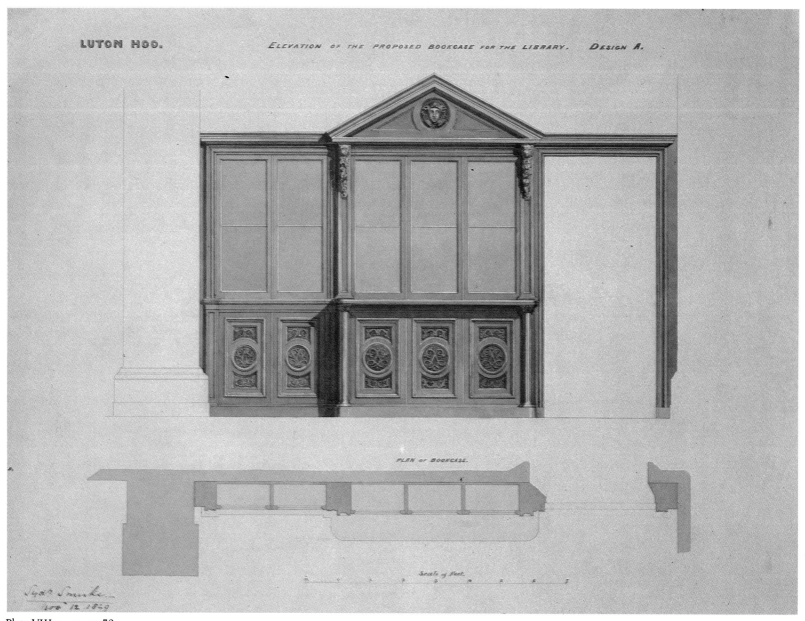

Plate VIII: see page 72

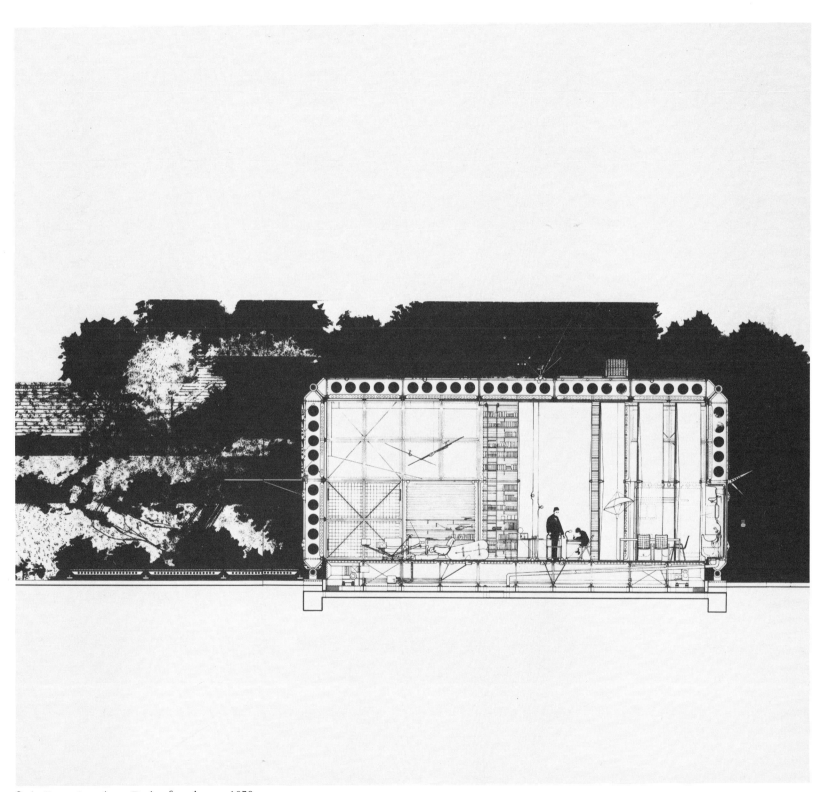

fig ix Foster Associates. Design for a house, 1979.

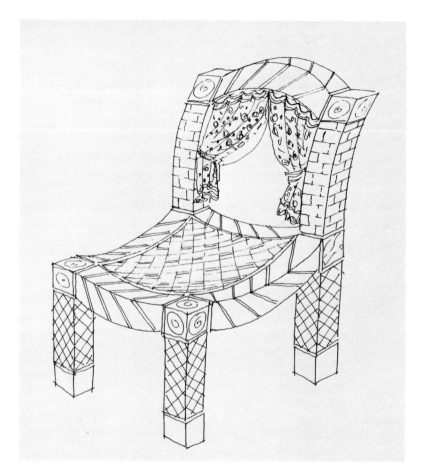

fig x John Outram (1934). Designs for His and Her chairs, 1979.

designs for furniture. But though furniture may sometimes resemble buildings (and buildings, furniture) the process of designing a building or a piece of furniture is related only analogically. While furniture may be seen as much a spatial creation as a building, the essential difference, putting aside function, is that of scale and its structural implications.

What the best architects have brought to furniture design is creativity informed by a training in design that, in the past, was not readily available to others. When travel was crucial to a would-be architect's education, it offered a stimulus and an understanding (often archaeologically derived) of both current and past design modes. The concerns that architects bring to the design of buildings may be reflected in their design of furniture and many formal and material innovations in furniture can be attributed to architects. The social context of design and in particular the problems associated with industrialisation and of, for instance, the effect of machine production on the life of the working man, were issues taken up by architect-

designers under the lead of Morris and Ruskin. E.W. Godwin, George Aitchison, R.W. Edis and others applied themselves to the sanitary reform of furniture and fittings, very necessary in the 1880s when the average life expectancy of the London poor was little more than forty years. Their efforts led the way for a much greater use of fitted furniture and furniture both fitted and freestanding tended towards a new simplicity.

Do architects, then, design the best furniture? It seems that, by and large, they do. Furniture-makers, inhibited by craft traditions, have usually been less adventurous than those outside the furniture trade. While (excepting the last fifty years or so) the amount of architect designed furniture actually produced has been slight, the radical innovations of the best examples have been enormously influential. The forms and details of many 'shop-bought' pieces though altered, adapted, diluted or vulgarized have their origins on an architect's drawing board.

'Architectural furniture' describes furniture, not necessarily designed by an architect, with obvious architectural features and is easily recognised but whether it is possible to attribute distinctive qualities to architect-designed furniture in general is doubtful. It can be monumentally large for 'there is a certain satisfaction to the eye to be gained by proportions which are in excess of mathematical requirements'[13] and 'outdoor scale brought indoors' describes William Kent's furniture as well as that of Salvin, Webb, Burges, Shaw and Waterhouse. For philosophic reasons as well as those of economy and convenience, a great deal of architect-designed furniture was (and is) joiner-made. The quality of 'archaeological exactitude' through a close study of the sources can certainly be attributed to some architect's furniture of the past but more often historical sources have been the stimulus to design: what marks the best architect-designed furniture is not copyism but invention. Not exclusive to architect-designed furniture is a quality, conscious or unconscious, of wit. It may be sophisticated or naive but astonishingly is scarcely absent in any of the designs discussed here. It seems as though furniture design finds the architect at his happiest.

1. *In The City and Country Builder's and Workman's Treasury of Designs,* 1740.

2. ibid. p.23

3. *Builder,* XIX, 1861, p.290

4. *Treatise on the Decorative Part of Civil Architecture,* 1791, pp.98,99

5. J.C. Loudon, *The Encyclopaedia of Cottage, Farm and Villa Architecture,* 1833, p.1039

6. J. Gloag, *Mr Loudon's England,* 1970, p.158

7. *Studio,* CXII, 1937, pp.266-75

8. J. Gloag, 'English furniture in the later twentieth century' *Connoisseur,* CC, 1979, p.248

9. R. Banham, 'Design by Choice', *Architectural Review,* CXXX, 1961, p.43

10. E. Goldfinger, *British Furniture Today,* 1951, p.6

11. From notes supplied by J. Outram

12. *Furniture in the House of Lords, a Report by the Victoria and Albert Museum,* 1974

13. C.F.A. Voysey, 'Ideas in Things', *The Arts Connected with Building,* J. Raffles Davison (ed.), 1909, p.120

Illustrations

The drawings reproduced here are all, except for fig. ii (Victoria and Albert Museum) and figs. ix and x (architect's own collection) in the Drawings Collection of the Royal Institute of British Architects. Published designs (figs. iii, iv, vii) are from the Library of the Royal Institute of British Architects.

Size of drawings: measurements are given in millimetres, height before width.

Size of furniture: where drawings are to scale, measurements in feet and inches are given, height before width before depth.

Inscriptions on drawings are given in italic type.

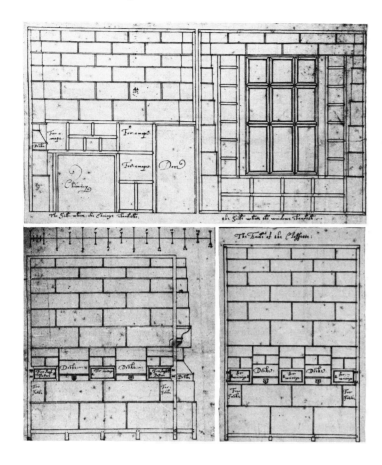

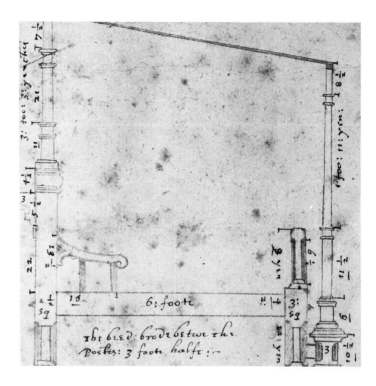

John Smythson (*d.* 1634)

2. Design for a bed, *c.*1600. Pencil, dimensions in
sepia pen (110 x 100) *h.* 6ft 9½ins *w.* 3ft 6ins
l. 6ft.

John Smythson was the son of Robert Smythson
and like his father he worked first as a mason, later
helping Robert in his architectural and surveying
practice. Bolsolver Castle was John's chief work. His
design for a bed is the earliest known surviving
English furniture designs and poses some
interesting problems. From the dimensions marked
on the drawing the bedstock (or bed frame) is 6 feet
long and 3½ feet wide and stands clear of the end
posts which are 4 feet 11½ inches high. The head
posts are 6 feet 9½ inches, that is 1 foot 10 inches
higher than the end posts. The resulting sloped
canopy suggests either a bed designed to fit under a
sloping roof or a travelling or field bed that is
dismountable. The bolts that hold the bedstock
together would have helped in dismantling the bed
but if it is indeed a field bed it might have been
more practical not to have detached end posts. The
armrest (not found in any surviving contemporary
examples) would have been very useful, while the
purpose of the bracket halfway up the head post can
only be guessed at. If it were to support a
candlestick then great care would need to be taken
not to set alight the headcloth, valances and
curtains.

Robert Smythson (1534 or 1535-1614)

1. Design for a closet, *c.*1600. Sepia pen (160 x 280,
170 x 155, 160 x 110) *scale*: approx. 1in to 2ft 4ins
h. 14ft 6ins *w.* 13ft, 13ft, 13ft and 11ft.

These elevations, despite some dimensional
discrepancies, appear to be a single design for the
four walls of a *closette* or small room. *Deskes* or
reading slopes, cupboards for *Loose Papers* and
writings, compartments for *Incke*, hanging spaces for
maps and shelves, presumably intended for books
and documents, suggest a combined library and
business room for one of Smythson's noble patrons.
The shelf compartments, diminishing as they rise,
correspond to the size of books that by 1600 were
published in formats ranging from sextodecimo to
folio. The unconventional and structurally illogical
staggered arrangement of the shelves is reminiscent
of stone coursing. Indeed, Smythson though later
described as an 'Architector & Survayor' began his
career as a mason and went on to become one of
the creators of the Elizabethan style, designing
Wollaton Hall, Worksop Manor and Hardwick Hall.

John Webb (1611-1672)

3. Unexecuted design for a bed and alcove for the bed chamber of Charles II at Greenwich Palace, 1665. Pen (290 x 445) Bed *h.* 9ft *w.* 7ft, alcove *h.* 14ft 6ins *w.* 14ft 2½ ins.

Vardy, who engraved this design in *Some Designs of Mr Inigo Jones . . .* (1744) as plate 4, misattributed it to Webb's master, from whose hand no furniture designs have survived. The notion of a state bed in an alcove protected by a balustrade was borrowed from France, and so was the form of the bed itself. Webb's scenic use of palm trees for the bed alcove probably derives from his masque designs and may be an allusion to Solomon. The exotic character of the bedroom seems at first to bear little relationship to Webb's architecture. But a comparison of his innovatory use of a giant Corinthian order to articulate the long façades on the east and north of the west wing at Greenwich, reveals a subtle correspondence. Thus Webb's palm trees grow out of Corinthian columns and flank doors in a way that echoes the arrangement of the exterior. His designs for the decoration of the King's private apartments at Greenwich are full of nicely-judged allusive details by which notions of patriotism, sovereignity and other qualities are conveyed as, for example, in the lion and unicorn capitals, the carved figures of Liberality and Magnanimity upon a *sopraporte*, and a ceiling design that contains an allegory of the Four Continents dominated by the Royal Navy, while symbols of chastity and conjugal fidelity enrich the mouldings of the King's bedchamber. Except for some chimneypieces none of Webb's designs for the interiors at Greenwich were used, though Vardy was to base his design for Lord Spencer's room at Spencer House, London, on Webb's design shown here.

William Talman (1650-1719)

4. Designs for furniture for a house at Thames Ditton, Surrey, c. 1699. Pen and wash (details from an album, 520 x 740) *scale*: 1 in to 5ft Large bed *h.* 11ft *w.* 6ft, small bed *h.* 7ft 6ins *w.* 5ft, garden chair *h.* 6ft 9ins *w.* 4ft.

Soon after William III's accession to the throne in 1689, William Talman secured the posts of Comptroller of Works and Deputy Superintendent of the Royal Gardens. A large part of his official work was concerned with the gardens and with the interior of the new building at Hampton Court Palace. Around 1699 Talman seems to have conceived the idea of building for himself a house at Ditton on the side of the Thames opposite Hampton Court Palace. The designs for this house, together with another scheme by William's son John, have also been thought to be unexecuted proposals for a Trianon (an informal retreat from the rigours of court life) for the King. But the newly discovered evidence of land deeds show that the site belonged to Talman. Thought of as a royal residence, the eleven-bay house with its formally laid-out gardens and double avenue of trees leading across the river to the Palace itself seems modest enough. Viewed as the architect's own house, the scheme begins to seem rather presumptuous. The motto on the frieze of the pedimented entrance, 'Vito Superba Civium Limina' — I avoid the thresholds of the proud and powerful — a free rendering of part of Horace's second Epode — is quite appropriate for a country retreat.

Talman's final design was drawn out in some detail and the longitudinal section shows the kind of decoration that was proposed. The elaborate chimneypieces, including a corner chimneypiece in the principal bedchamber, and the beds, rely upon contemporary French sources, in particular on the work of the Hugenot architect and designer, Daniel Marot. The gardens of Talman's house included a water garden, parterre, bowling alley, orchards and a garden enclosed by a tall, architecturally treated hedge, of a type sometimes aptly known as 'King William's fortifications'. This had alcoves in front of some of which were placed garden seats of throne-like character — another example, possibly, of *lese-majesté*. The scallop shell and fretted back, festoons and scrolly arms and legs were all motifs freely borrowed from Marot's engraved designs.

On the 19th of March 1702, King William died and Talman, whose arrogance and intransigence had made him many enemies, lost his official appointments. The house by the Thames was never realised and the site was sold to George London, a highly successful nurseryman and gardener.

William Kent (?1685-1748)

5. Design for a state barge for Frederick, Prince of Wales, 1732. Pen and sepia wash (hull plan and elevation 330 x 520, details of poop and statehouse 305 x 470) *scale*: approx. 1 in to 3 ft Statehouse *h.* 6 ft 6 ins *w.* 6 ft.

Kent, who is said to have begun as a coach painter, went on to become a history painter and interior decorator before turning to architecture, landscape gardening and the design of sculpture, silver plate, stage scenery, and furniture.

His first commission from Frederick, Prince of Wales was the building of Kew House in 1731. Soon after this Kent was entrusted with the design for a state barge. He chose (or more likely was advised) to use a traditional wherry hull form with its long, narrow and shallow lines. Kent's plan and elevation show the hull 57 feet long and about 5 feet 8 inches wide but, as executed, the clinker-built barge was 63 feet long and with a beam of 6 feet 6 inches. Kent at first provided six rowlocks a side for twelve oarsmen. They must have had a hard time rowing such a vessel in tidal waters for at some stage, it seems, the barge was lengthened by 8 feet and the number of rowlocks increased to eleven on the starboard side and ten on the port, allowing for twenty one oarsmen in all.

The splendid carving on the barge was done by James Richards who had succeeded Grinling Gibbons as Master Carver in Wood to the Crown. It was built at John Hall's boatyard opposite Whitehall and launched at Chelsea Hospital on 13 July 1732 when the Queen, Prince Frederick and the five princesses, accompanied by the 'Officers and Ladies in Waiting of the Court in another Barge, and a Set of Musick in the third Barge... proceeded to Somerset House'[1] The accounts made out to joiner, carver, gilder, mercer, laceman, upholsterer, sailmaker, oar-maker, glassman and locksmith as well as tailor, hatmaker, hosier and silversmith for the oarsmen's and barge-master's uniforms, came to £1,174 14s.

Kent's design for the barge is consistent with his designs for furniture, that is, 'rich, florid and monumental'[2] with large-scale ornament and much gilding. Its nautical function suggested the riot of mermaids, dolphins, sealions, porpoises, seaweed-like foliage, scallop shells, fish masks and oak-with-acorn festoons that decorate the royal barge. A Vitruvian scroll or wave moulding runs along the gunwale and the ribs of the statehouse have fishscale ornament while inside are panels painted with sea shells, seaweed and coral. A final, felicitous touch was the scaley caps and seaweedy lace decoration of the watermen's uniforms.

After Prince Frederick's death in 1751, his barge continued in use until 1849. It is now at the National Maritime Museum, Greenwich.

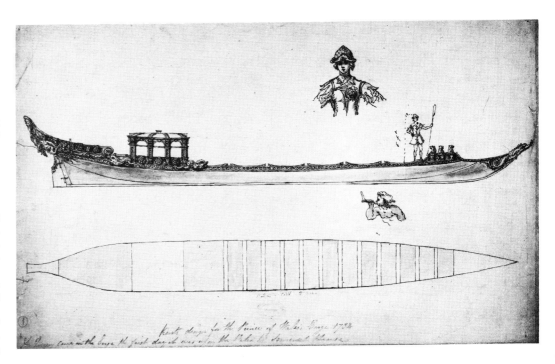

John Vardy (d. 1765)

6. Design for a double chaise-longue, c. 1755-61. Pen with pink, yellow and grey washes (430 x 490) *scale*: 1in to 1ft *w.* 13ft 9ins *see* Plate I, p.19.

7. Design for a pier-glass and table, for the 5th Duke of Bolton, Hackwood Park, Hampshire, c. 1761-3. Pen with grey and blue washes (460 x 295) *scale*: 15/16in to 1ft Pier-glass *h.* 7ft ins *w.* 5ft 5ins, table *h.* 2ft 11½ins *w.* 5ft 1in.

8. (*attributed to* Vardy) Designs for garden seats in Kensington Gardens, London, c. 1754-61. Sepia pen and wash (340 x 480) Circular seat *h.* 3ft 4ins *diam.* 6ft 1in, bench *h.* 3ft 6ins *w.* 7ft *d.* 1ft 11ins.

Vardy's best known building is Spencer House, Green Park, London designed in the correct Neo-Palladianism that he learnt during his employment at the Office of Works. Vardy's furniture designs are either in the manner of his mentor William Kent or in a Rococo style that reveals a sound understanding of French *rocaille*. It has been suggested that Vardy had a share in a family joinery business.[3] Certainly his brother Thomas was a carver and it seems very likely that John supplied him with furniture designs.

It is not known for whom Vardy designed this elaborately canopied double chaiselongue (fig. 6). The drawing is one of several by Vardy, dated between 1755 and 1761, that came from Milton Abbey. In 1752 the Abbey was sold to a local man, Joseph Damers, who acquired also an Irish peerage, then an English one and then an earldom. He did not achieve a dukedom though he did marry a duke's daughter. Thus the ducal coronet sketchily drawn-in above a fictive coat of arms on the canopy is unlikely to refer to Lord Milton. Perhaps the chaise-longue with carved owls was commissioned by the 3rd Duke of Devonshire, whose arms include 'three owls of the field' and for whom William Kent designed a mirror and side table bearing carved owls. Or perhaps it was for the 5th Duke of Bolton whose family name was Powlett. On the other hand it might have been designed for another of Vardy's patrons, Sir Thomas Hayles of Howletts in Kent. The owls with outspread wings at either end of the chaise-longue are more probably intended as attributes of Sleep and since they are nocturnal and this is, after all, a day bed, that seems very likely. The clocks they surmount symbolise, of course, Temperance: a timely reminder to the occupants, whoever they were, of this unusual double chaise-longue.

7

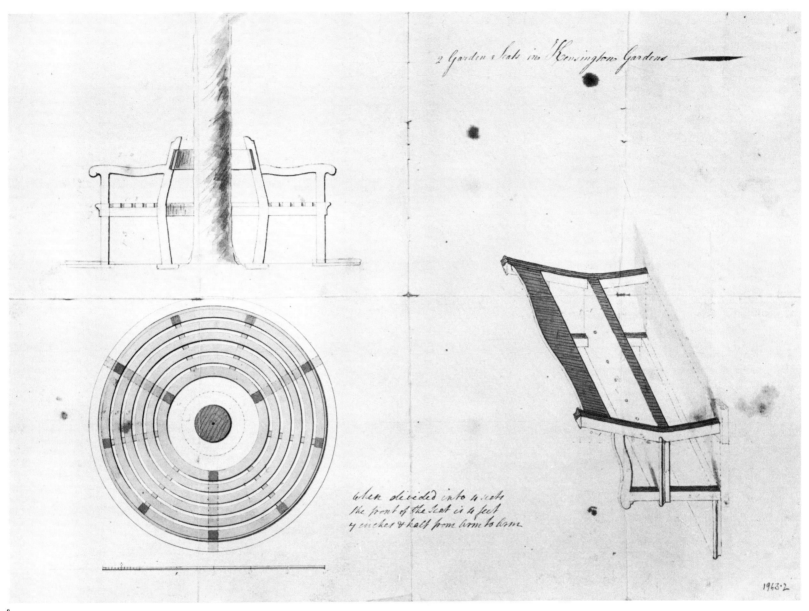

2 Garden Seats in Kensington Gardens

when divided into 4 seats the front of the seat is 4 feet 4 inches & half from arm to arm

1963·2

8

Between 1761 and 1763 Vardy was employed at Hackwood Park on various alterations to the house, and the elaborately Rococo gilt wood table and pier-glass that was designed, with other furniture, for the house remains there still (fig. 7).

For several years (1754-1761) Vardy was Clerk of the Works at Kensington Palace, the Gardens of which were private though the Broad Walk was open to 'all respectably dressed persons' on Saturdays throughout the summer months. Details of the draughtsmanship suggest that Vardy made the designs for a circular seat to encompass a tree and for a bench seat for Kensington Gardens (fig. 8). Their rational design with such details as the rain-shedding caps to the bench uprights and the leak-holes in the seat could hardly be bettered.

John Sanderson (d. 1774)

9. Design for the Great Room, Kimberley Hall, Norfolk for Sir John Wodehouse Bt, 1770. Pen with grey and yellow washes (520 x 540) *scale:* approx. 1in to 3ft room 25ft x 20ft 4ins *see* Plate II, p.17.

10. (*attributed to* Sanderson)
Design for a bookcase, possibly for the 1st Baron Lyttleton, Hagley Hall, Worcestershire, *c.* 1758. Sepia pen and wash (195 x 315) *scale:* approx. ½in to 1ft *h.* 9ft 6ins *w.* 17ft.

The design for the Great Room at Kimberley Hall (fig. 9) is bound into an album with other designs for the interiors, all apparently prepared by Sanderson between 1761 and 1770. In the late 1750s he had assisted Thomas Prowse, a country gentleman and amateur architect, in the remodelling of the house earlier built by William Talman.

Sanderson was a competent Neo-Palladian architect who occasionally revealed a flair for Rococo decoration. In his scheme for the Great Room, ceiling, doors, windows, dado and cornice are organised with Palladian correctness but the spaces between are a riot of Rococo efflorescence. With a liberality that often distinguishes designers of the Rococo, Sanderson offers alternative decorative treatments for each of three walls: the fourth is left unadorned. Above the chimneypiece are figures of Victory and Fame holding a crown of laurels over the profile medallion of John Wodehouse, victor of Agincourt. On either side, the severely rectilinear frames of the mirrors are enveloped by ornament that threatens to engulf the furniture below. On the left, there is a sofa and on the other side what is either an impossibly long-legged sofa or else a table with, it seems, a squab on it. Another wall elevation has console tables of differing character: one is Rococo, the other has coin-patterned tapering legs. None of the furniture, if it was made, has survived at Kimberley and of Sanderson's stucco decoration for what is now the music room, only the ceiling design was, apparently, executed.

The elevation of a bookcase (fig. 10) is neither signed, dated nor inscribed but the design and draughtsmanship suggest an attribution to John Sanderson. And if the statue of Shakespeare on the right is after that made by Roubiliac for David Garrick in 1758 (the left-hand one is probably after Scheemakers's monument of 1740) then a *post-quem* date is established. Of the three known commissions that Sanderson was involved in at this time, Hagley Hall is the most likely location for this piece of furniture. The library, with other rooms, was destroyed by fire in 1925 but carefully restored soon afterwards. The present white-painted bookcases have broken pediments with Scheemaker's busts of Shakespeare, Spenser, Milton and Dryden

10

bequeathed by Alexander Pope to Lord Lyttleton in 1744. Lyttleton — politician, poet, historian and patron of literature — was also a Man of Taste. For both the landscaping (begun ten years before the house) and the architecture of Hagley Hall he sought advice and designs from a number of friends, all more or less amateur architects. Sanderson Miller provided the final design and he was helped by Thomas Prowse and, as working architect, John Sanderson. As at Kimberley Hall, Sanderson's rôle was to draw out the plans and elevations and, apparently, to design the 'finishings' including much of the Rococo plasterwork as well as the library fittings. The design shown here for a bookcase (with another not illustrated) may be an alternative design to the executed one. It accords with the Palladianism of the house but is freer and has, characteristically, a Rococo touch in the brackets beneath the statues.

9

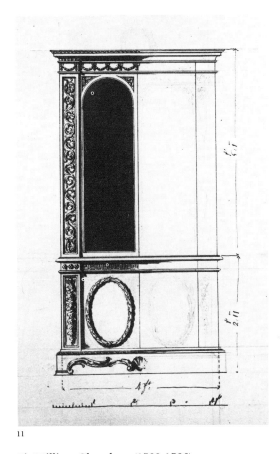

11

12

Sir William Chambers (1723-1796)

11. Design for a bookcase for the library at The Hoo, Hertfordshire for Thomas Brand, *c.* 1760-64. Pen and wash with some pencil (485 x 330) *scale*: 1in to 1ft *h.* 8ft *w.* 4ft 4ins.

12. Design for a looking-glass, *c.* 1770. Pen with grey and blue washes and some pencil (260 x 345) *scale*: 3ins to 1ft *h.* 2ft 10¼ins *w.* 1ft 8ins.

The Hoo, a house built during the Protectorate (and demolished in 1957) was altered and added to by Chambers. A scholarly eclectic, Chambers designed his major buildings, such as Somerset House, in an English Palladian style refined by French Neo-Classicism using a variety of styles including Moorish and Chinese for his slighter works. His ceiling and chimneypiece designs for The Hoo were made in a conservative manner in keeping with the Artisan Mannerist architecture of the house. Chambers's design for a bookcase for the library (fig. 11), meticulously related to the height of skirting, dado and ceiling, was entirely of its time using Neo-Palladian, Neo-Classical and Rococo motifs.

Chambers's design (fig. 12) in a Rococo style, for an oval standing looking-glass decorated with acanthus leaves, scallop shells and a coronet has, despite the draperies, a masculine air that suggests powdered wig, dressing room and male vanity. It may have been for the architect's own use since the drawing is one of many bound into an album of decorative details for houses in Berners Street, St Marylebone, London — a speculative development that included a house for the architect.

13

James Stuart (1713-1788)

13a & b. Design for the decoration and furniture of a room, *c.* 1757. Pen and coloured washes (both, 190 x 150) *see* Plate III, p.23 (13b.)

14. Design for a side-table, *c.* 1757. Pen with yellow, orange and grey washes, some pencil (270 x 180).

Stuart's publication (with Nicholas Revett) of *The Antiquities of Athens* (volume I, 1762) earned him the sobriquet of 'Athenian' Stuart as well as considerable fame and a number of commissions. Indolence prevented him from making many substantial architectural designs and his work was mostly confined to interior decoration and garden buildings. Stuart's real importance lies in his introduction of Greek architecture to England. He designed the first Greek Revival building (the Doric

temple at Hagley Park, 1758-9) and his interiors and furniture are the earliest fully Neo-Classical examples in this country.

The room for which Stuart drew these elevations has not yet been identified. It is possible that the design (fig. 13) with its charming cornice decoration of putti and festoons remained unexecuted. Stuart's use in one of the elevations of a large semicircular arched motif is characteristic of his work. The settee with its straight, turned legs is very similar to one in the sub-hall at Kedleston Hall and Stuart's unused designs[4] for the saloon at Kedleston have many of the motifs (figures with festoons, dado rail with Vitruvian scroll, wreath ornaments) to be found in the elevations shown here. It is tempting to associate them with Kedleston and in particular with Lady Caroline Curzon's dressing room for which Adam

was later to design a combined bookcase and clothes press. This was after he had ousted Stuart, for their patron Sir Nathaniel Curzon was a man apt to change his mind. Matthew Brettingham the Elder, the first architect of the house, was replaced after a year by James Paine who in turn was replaced by the ubiquitous Adam who took over the house, its interior and the park.

Adam, on his Grand Tour, had ventured as far as Split in Dalmatia but had not visited Greece. Thus Greece was a touchy subject with him and he adopted a heavily sarcastic manner to Stuart calling him the 'Archipeligan Architect' and ridiculing his work. Of Stuart's designs for Kedleston, Robert Adam wrote to his brother James, that Stuart did not hesitate to cut '3 feet off the length of the best pictures and 2 feet off the height of the others' in order to make them fit his decorative schemes. And that he (Stuart) proposed 'tables 2 foot square in a room 50 feet long', a comment that might refer to Stuart's design for a side-table, the location of which is not known (fig. 14). Certainly his design for a chimneypiece for the saloon at Kedleston had the same lion's paw feet with studded 'anklets' and ribboned wreaths of vine leaves as the table: decorative motifs derived from the purest Antique sources. But then the same motifs were used for another chimneypiece for the dining room at Nuneham Park, a Palldian villa (1756-64) for the first Earl Harcourt by Stiff Leadbetter and for which Stuart designed the interior.

The design for the candelabrum that stands on the table (fig. 14) is based upon the classical tripod and may be derived from the tripod of the Choragic Monument of Lysicrates published in *The Antiquities of Athens*. The tripod became a much used motif in Neo-Classical interiors and furniture and its introduction by Stuart underlines the archaeological correctness that gives his work its distinctive quality. The inclusion of urns and plaques in his designs seems to have been an important source of inspiration for Josiah Wedgwood.

14

(Attributed to) **William Porden** (1755-1822)

Designs for the decoration of a bedroom and dressing room, Aldewark Hall, Yorkshire, *c.* 1792.

15. Bed alcove. Sepia pen with sepia, green and yellow washes (detail from sheet, 535 x 690) *scale*: approx. 1in to 2ft 6ins Bed *h.* 8ft 7in *w.* 3ft 4ins *l.* 5ft 4ins.

16. Dressing table. Sepia pen and wash (detail from sheet 690 x 535) *scale*: approx. 1in to 2ft 6ins *h.* 2ft 6ins *w.* 4ft 6ins.

Marriage often precipitates new building work and Francis Ferrand Foljambe's marriage to Mary Thornhaugh in 1774 seems to have occasioned the decoration by James Wyatt of the reception rooms at Aldewark Hall[5] (built 1720 and demolished 1899). Porden was then a pupil in Wyatt's office and on Foljambe's second marriage in 1792 to Lady Mary Lumley (he had been widowed two years before) was asked to design new stables and farm buildings as well as, it has been assumed, the decoration and furniture of a bedroom and dressing room.[6]

The bedroom was given a bed alcove (fig. 15) flanked by closets on either side and the alternative decorative treatments for the alcove were derived from Robert Adam via James Wyatt but done with a coarse vigour alien to both. For Lady Mary Foljambe's dressing-room, used also as a sitting room and slightly larger than her bedroom, Porden provided a sofa alcove and designed a concave-fronted dressing table (fig. 16). This has a mirror surmounted by a bow, quiver of arrows and a sprig of myrtle — the attributes of Venus and a pleasant compliment to the new bride.

15

16

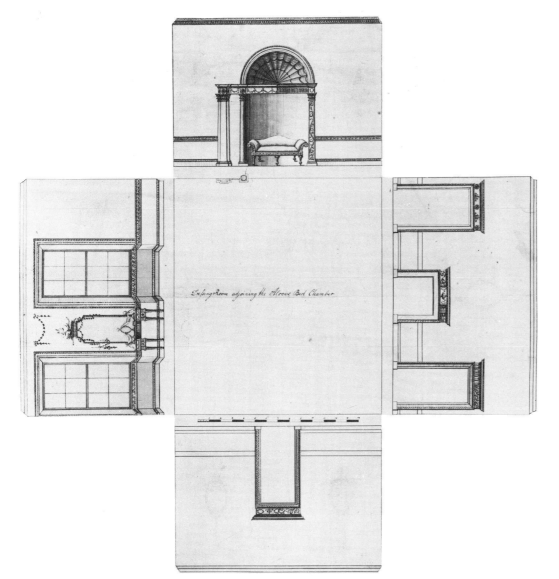

18

Joseph Bonomi (1739-1808)

17. Design for the decoration of a drawing room for Mrs Elizabeth Montagu, 22 Portman Square, London, *c.* 1782. Pen and wash (250 x 515) *scale*: ½in to 1ft Room 33ft 6ins x 21ft.

18. Design for the dining room and its furniture, Lambton Hall (now Castle), County Durham, for the executors of William John Lambton, 1800. Pen and watercolour (450 x 650) *see* Plate IV, p.24.

Mrs Elizabeth Montagu (1720-1800), authoress, hostess and by 1775, a rich widow, decided in that year (or soon after) to build a town house on the corner of the newly laid-out Portman Square. Her architect was James 'Athenian' Stuart and it was perhaps because of his unreliability and failure to provide detailed drawings that she employed Joseph Bonomi to design some of the rooms at Montagu House. The literary breakfasts, evening conversation parties and receptions that made Mrs Montagu the leading hostess to the intellectual society of London required a number of reception rooms. The grandest of these was the 'Great Room' or saloon by Bonomi (destroyed, with the rest of the house, by bombing, 1941). He also prepared designs for a gallery and for a drawing room that were not executed (fig. 17). These share the Corinthian columns and segmental ceilings with *cinquecento* decoration of the Great Room. The massive

17

character of these rooms, the vigorous modelling, emphatic rhythm and the sombre rendering of his drawings emphasise the 'Italian or modernised Roman character'[7] of these designs. There is little of the Adam influence that he might have absorbed while working for several years in that office after his arrival from Rome in 1767. Bonomi's oval mirrors with candelabra (placed inconveniently high) have the same qualities as his decoration while his sofa, which shares the same scallop shell ornament as the mirrors, is plain and understated and clearly not intended to compete with the other elements of the room.

In 1795 Bonomi was asked to rebuild Lambton Hall but unhappily his patron died from consumption within two years and Bonomi's design was abandoned. Until 1801, a modified scheme of additions was carried out and if this included the dining room, it was swept away in the course of subsequent rebuilding. Nor has any Bonomi-designed furniture survived.

The design for the dining room (fig. 18) was exhibited at the Royal Academy in 1800, the same year that Bonomi was elected as an Academician. The strikingly drawn perspective shows shafts of sunlight filtering through tall, round-arched windows onto the austerely boarded floor and massive Neo-Classical furniture. The design suggests the asceticism of a monastic refectory rather than the game larder pleasures of a North Country land-owner. The tall, vaulted ceiling springs from a mannered entablature derived from Vignola and the lines of vaulting are emphasised by a vigorous husk moulding. Ceiling, dado and architraves are washed a pale stone colour, the walls are greenish-grey, while skirting and doors are of the same dark, figured wood as the furniture. Severely Neo-Classical in design, the dining table has fluted, tapered legs of a large square section and the sideboard, flanked by pedestals bearing urns, has the same sort of support. The curious tables beneath the windows have waisted, taper legs of circular section. Their half-elliptical form allows for two to be pushed together to make a larger table: a practical arrangement when few people were eating or when there were more than the twenty-two that could be comfortably seated at the main table, and useful too, as additional serving tables. The idealized, Neo-Classical landscape of the wall paintings was suggested, no doubt, by the nearby River Wear.

Henry Holland (1745-1806)

19. Design for a pier table for the library of Woburn Abbey, Bedfordshire, for the 5th Duke of Bedford, *c.* 1787-93. Pen (375 x 260) *scale*: approx. 1½ins to 1ft *h.* 3ft 0½in *w.* 3ft 8½ins *d.* 1ft 7½ins.

20. Design for an ornamental stand to support a lamp, *c.* 1800. Pen (375 x 260) *scale*: 4ins to 1ft *h.* 2ft 2ins *diam.* 2ft, plinth *h.* 4ins *w.* 2ft 7ins.

21. Design for the ornamental casing of a stove for the Upper Octagon, Carlton House, London for George, Prince of Wales, 1794. Pen (180 x 120) *scale*: 1in to 2ft 3ins *h.* 9ft 8ins *w.* 5ft *d.* 1ft 9ins.

The design for the pier table (fig. 19) and for an ornamental stand (fig. 20) are two of many working drawings re-drawn by draughtsmen in Holland's office and bound into a record book. These designs are mostly for details of interior decoration carried out from the mid-1780s until 1800, a period when Holland's highly personal Neo-Classical style with its strongly Gallic flavour was achieving its fullest development.

From 1787 Holland received much employment from Francis, 5th Duke of Bedford (1765-1802). In particular, the architect remodelled part of Woburn Abbey, made some additions and designed a number of park and farm buildings including the Chinese Dairy. Within the house he formed a new library, or rather library suite, along most of the south range. To the west he placed an ante-library leading into the Great Library beyond which was another library room. It was remarkable that a patron who confessed to having scarcely read a book until he was twenty four should have required such handsome accommodation. Every wall received fitted bookcases and between the windows were placed pier tables, also built-in. Holland, more than any other architect at this time, seems to have made a practice of designing pieces of furniture as architectural fixtures. The use of pier tables as storage space and to maintain the consistency of a book-lined room is typical of Holland's search for 'purity, precision, perfect sequence'[8], as evident in his furniture designs as in the *enfilade* planning of the library.

The pier tables were modified in execution so that instead of the space for duodecimo (very small) books indicated on the drawing, the sides were closed and the front used for folio books. The design is simple; the only embellishments are the tapering reeded legs set into recessed corners, a device found in French furniture of this date. Like the bookcases, the pier tables were painted white with some details picked out in gold. The library, its fittings and other furniture designed by Holland exists still and is at present among the private rooms not shown to the public.

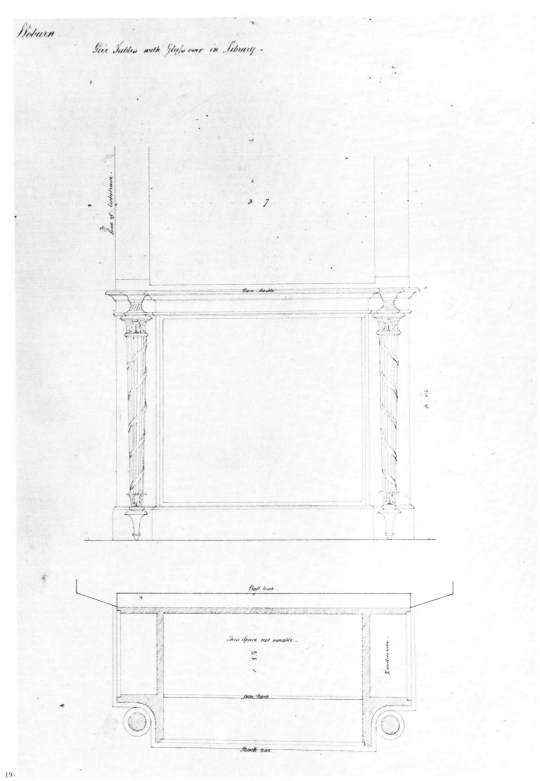

19.

Holland seems to have had a gift for extracting the best out of the men who worked for him. In about 1789 he took Charles Heathcote Tatham into his office and five years later helped to finance the young man's visit to Italy. In return Tatham supplied his master with sketches, casts and fragments of Roman, Grecian and Egyptian ornament bought from Roman dealers or sketched from specimens in the Vatican Museum. It was from Tatham's discoveries that Holland derived the large-scale animal forms used by him as supports or terminals in his furniture designs. Such motifs were widely taken up after the publication of Tatham's drawings in 1799-1800.

The most striking element in the part-elevation of a lamp standard is the chimera — a fire-breathing monster with a lion's head, serpent's tail and eagle's wings. The design shows the stand to have a tapered central pillar, chastely decorated, with a circular base that with the (presumably) three flanking chimerae supports a circular top on which rests an oil lamp whose design echoes that of the main pillar. The chimerae seem to be structurally superfluous and despite the adaptable anatomy of such a beast, the clumsy support issuing from the neck demonstrates the problems involved when animal forms are used.

Holland's practice was large and his patrons influential. None more so than George, Prince of Wales who, when he came of age on 12 August 1783, was given Carlton House as his London residence. By the end of the year his private architect Henry Holland was in charge of the reconstruction of the house and during the next thirteen years designed a sequence of rooms that Horace Walpole declared 'the most perfect in Europe'. At the centre was an octagonal vestibule top-lit by a lantern in the centre of a fan-vaulted ceiling and with a gallery or Upper Octagon.

Hundreds of the decorative details of Carlton House were copied into a series of office record books of which the RIBA Drawings Collection has Nos 8 and 13. Among the details are a number for the Octagon including three designs for stoves. The elegant vase stove for the Upper Octagon (fig. 21) was not apparently among the items re-used at Windsor Castle and Buckingham Palace after the demolition of Carlton House (1827-8).

For the marble and plaster casing for a stove, probably in cast-iron, Holland used details taken from the architectural decoration of the Octagon, completed a few years before. Thus the wreath on the front of the stove appears elsewhere and the mask of Apollo, the sun god was used for the *center pannell in Soffit of Passage . . . from the Upper Octagon*. The ram's heads, grotesques and sphinxes that together with the tripod pedestal form of the middle stage of the stove are reminiscent of the work of Robert Adam.

The slow combustion stove was introduced in the mid-18th century and was generally disguised as something quite else (a trophy or a suit of armour) or else designed as part of the decorations of the room it stood in. The 'vase' on the 'pedestal' is a flue that creates a down-draught. Holland shows no opening and this must have occurred on the other side of the wall against which the stove was placed, thus allowing for discreet and invisible servicing.

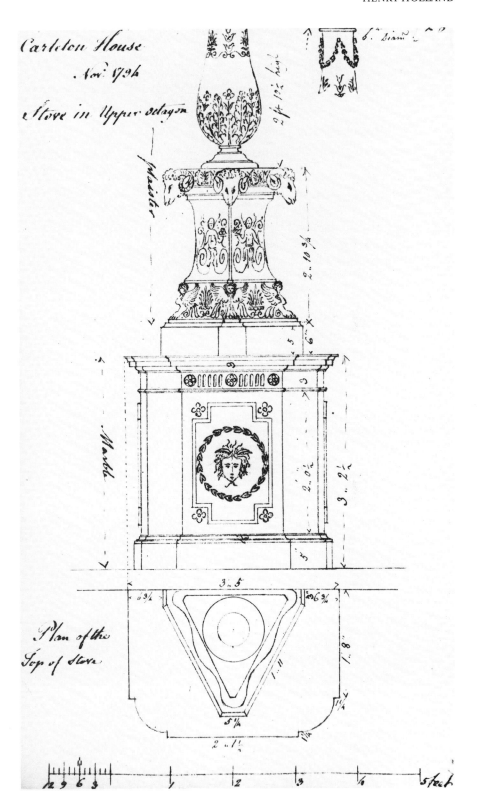

21

Samuel Pepys Cockerell (1743-1827) & Thomas Daniell (1749-1840)

22. Design for an oil lamp and pedestal for the hall of Sezincote House, Gloucestershire, for Sir Charles Cockerell Bt., 1809. Pen and wash with pencil (260 x 410), pen and pencil (330 x 535) *scale*: ¾in to 1ft and full size Pedestal *h.* 8ft 8ins *w.* 4ft 3ins *d.* 2ft 2ins, oil lamp *h.* 1ft 2ins *w.* 1ft 1in *d.* 9¼ins.

In 1795 Colonel John Cockerell bought Sezincote House near Moreton-in-Marsh. He died three years later and left it to his sister and his younger brothers Charles and Samuel Pepys Cockerell. Charles bought out his co-legatees and by about 1805, having amassed a fortune through his service in the East India Company, was ready to re-model and enlarge the existing house. The design for the new work was entrusted to his architect brother. An Indian style was thought to be the most appropriate for the nabob and S.P. Cockerell turned to Thomas Daniell, artist and traveller in India, for assistance. The decorative details of the exterior: the lattice panels, lacey multi-foiled arches, the *chattris* and *chujjas* were suggested by Daniell. Cockerell combined these exotic elements with a picturesque composition and skilful planning, producing a sensitive and original synthesis of Moghul and late Georgian classical architecture.

The interior (it has been much altered since) was designed in a restrained Neo-Classical style but there was one object at least which was inspired by India. A five-branched oil lamp was designed for the hall and, flanked by doors leading to the staircase, stood opposite the entrance. Framed by a blank, pointed arch bisected by a date or palm tree (executed in plaster) and on a Grecian-style pedestal embellished by a panel depicting a scene from Indian life, stood a howdah-bearing elephant. From the floor of the howdah projected five lampholders with glass flues and the oil reservoir for these was contained within the howdah itself. Daniell seems to have drawn the front and side elevations of the oil lamp and pedestal; Cockerell the details of the lamp and oil reservoir. The ensemble is an endearing piece of design of which the pedestal and tree, but not the elephant oil lamp, have survived.

22

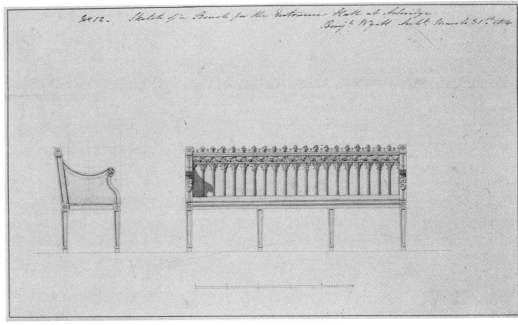

24

Thomas Cundy, Senior (1765-1825)

23. Alternative designs for a sideboard table,
c. 1815. Pencil and coloured washes (detail from
page 125 x 205) *scale:* ⅛in to 1ft *h.* 4ft 6ins *w.* 8ft
d. 2ft 3ins *see* Plate V, p.25.

Cundy was not an innovator. His designs for houses,
villas, lodges and cottages, executed in a
conventional Classical or Gothic or castle or rustic
style, had a pretty propriety that appealed to
unadventurous patrons. His alternative designs for
the sideboard table (one of many designs, most of
them architectural, in an office record book made by
Thomas Cundy, Junior (1790-1867) while employed
by his father) offer a mixture of contemporary motifs
with some that were fairly old fashioned. Sideboards
with drawers and cupboards were introduced in the
1780s but did not replace the sideboard table for
some time. The sarcophagus-like wine-cooler or
cellaret was an established form by 1815.

Benjamin Dean Wyatt (1775-1850)

24. Design for a hall settle for the entrance hall,
Ashridge Park, Hertfordshire for the 7th Earl of
Bridgewater, 1814. Pen with grey, brown and pink
washes (255 x 415) *scale:* 1in to 1ft *h.* 3ft 2½ins *w.* 7ft
d. 2ft 1in *see* Plate VI, p.26.

James Wyatt designed Ashridge Park in a castellated
Gothic style from 1807 until his death in 1813. His
eldest son Benjamin then continued the work,
completing the design of the entrance hall and great
staircase, and of the chapel.

The tall and narrow entrance hall that leads from
the porch to the staircase hall has a hammerbeam
roof and a 'rood screen' with a two-storey 'loft'. The
tracery, foliated moulding and cresting of the settle
are all faithfully derived from the architectural
decoration of the hall but applied to a Neo-Classical
form: 'Georgian bodies dressed up in Plantaganet
clothes' and the kind of thing that Pugin was to
fulminate against.

Furniture of a special character for halls and
corridors was introduced early in the 18th century
and Wyatt's designs conform to that type of strong,
plainly constructed seat intended for the use of
servants or strangers waiting on business. Neither
the settle nor the matching chairs nor indeed any of
the furniture designed by the Wyatts for Ashridge
has survived there.

Sir Robert Smirke (1780-1867)

25. Design for a fire screen/pier table, *c.* 1816. Pencil with grey and yellow washes (210 x 300) *scale:* approx. 1⅜in to 1ft *h.* 4ft *w.* 6ft.

Smirke's *Screen before a Fireplace serving as a Pier-table* is an unusual dual-purpose piece of furniture[9]. During the summer months it concealed the fireplace opening and, at the same time, provided an additional side-table. The semi-elliptical top is supported by four sprightly nymphs derived from Greek architectural sculpture. In order to emphasise the effect of weight and resistance upon these load-bearing maidens consideration must be given as to which leg should appear braced and which merely inclined. And here Smirke reverses a precedent such as the caryatids on the Erectheum. In an essay[10] he wrote at about this time, Smirke devoted several pages to 'The Caryatids', chivalrously asking 'what art, what ingenuity, can reconcile the mind to the idea of placing a beautiful female in a situation to which the strength of an horse is unequal?' For, 'some well executed figures have so lively an impression of human intellect, and corporeal animation, that it is impossible to look at the resemblance of so interesting a form, in such a state of sufference, without a painful sense of impropriety.' Happily, 'the figures which artists employ in this way . . . are now always represented so entirely at their ease that the spectator is in no danger from his sympathy for [the] sufferings of a fellow creature in distress. Their duty, indeed, appears to be really *lady's work* — evidently a pleasure rather than a toil'.

Similar nymphs are to be found in other of Smirke's designs of this period and suggest a date of about 1816 for the screen/table. The room for which it was designed has not been identified. Of the many commissions that Smirke carried out at this time, his remodelling of the library at Lansdowne House, London into a picture gallery suggests that as a possible location.

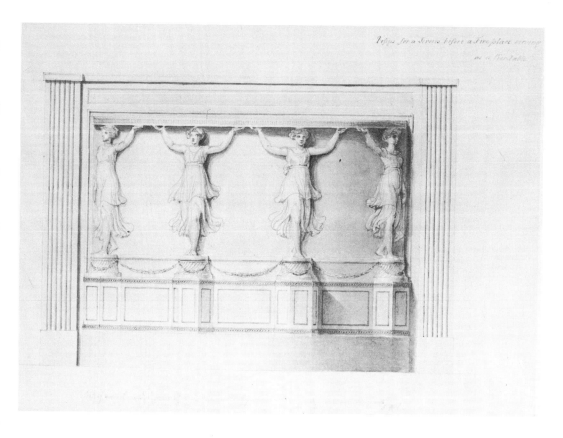

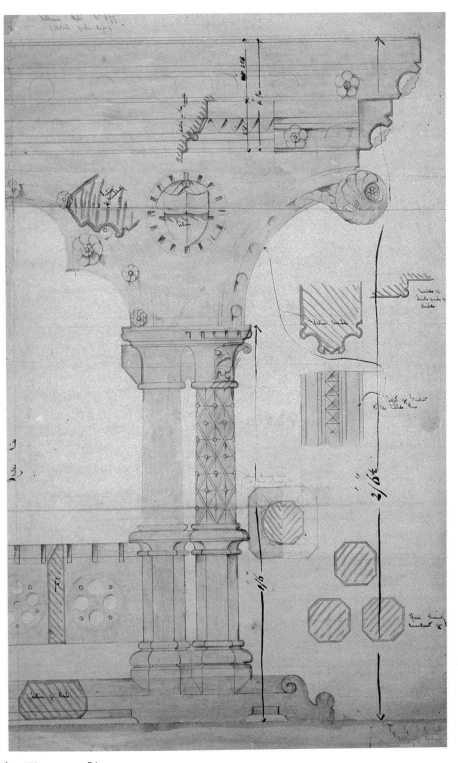

Plate IX: see page 74

Plate X: see page 75

Plate XI: see page 76

Plate XII: see page 79

26

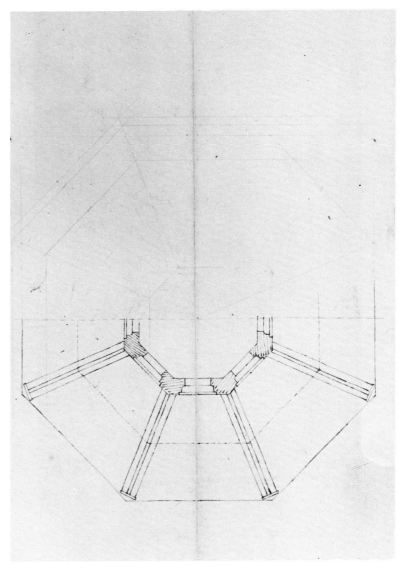

Sir Jeffry Wyatville (1766-1840)

26. Design for an octagonal porters' table for the entrance hall, Ashridge Park, Hertfordshire for the 7th Earl of Bridgewater, 1815. Sepia pen and wash with pencil additions (350 x 220) *scale*: 2ins to 1ft *h.* 2ft 6ins *w.* (as altered) 4ft.

27. Design for an octagonal table for the staircase hall, Ashridge Park, 1823. Pen and some pencil (745 x 555) *scale*: 1in to 1ft and full size *h.* 2ft 5ins *w.* 4ft.

Benjamin Dean Wyatt was briefly employed at Ashridge park after his father's death in 1813. The following year his cousin Jeffry (later Sir Jeffry Wyatville) took over. To a house already large (the front was over 400 feet long) was added a 100 foot wing containing the family apartments and beyond this an orangery, 150 feet long, was built. On the other side of the house, extensive stables and various estate buildings were added. Wyatville also designed some of the furniture including an octagonal porters' table for the entrance hall (fig. 26). A year before B.D. Wyatt had designed a bench and chair for the same hall (fig. 24). Wyatville used a font-like pedestal with trefoil arched openings and top

supported by brackets similar to those of the hammerbeam roof to the hall. Three, at least, of these tables were made and were slightly modified in execution so that, for example, the shield-shaped stops to the brackets were omitted. Octagonal-shaped tables are not common: Soane had designed a striking example in ebony and ivory for, it seems, the library at Stowe in about 1805 (now at the Art Gallery and Museum, Brighton). Wyatville seems to have liked that form for he designed another (fig. 27) for the staircase hall, in an 'Elizabethan' style. Like most of the so-called Elizabethan furniture that was to become increasingly popular, it included Jacobean and Stuart elements as well as nailhead decoration borrowed from Norman architecture — a favourite Wyatville motif.

Wyatville's interest in 'the manner of the days of Queen Elizabeth' showed itself long before the Elizabethan revival got under way in the 1830s. Early in the century he added to Longleat House, carefully reproducing the detail of the exterior and using some Elizabethan details in the interiors. And in about 1815, he designed furniture of an Elizabethan character for the Duke of Bedford's cottage at Endsleigh.

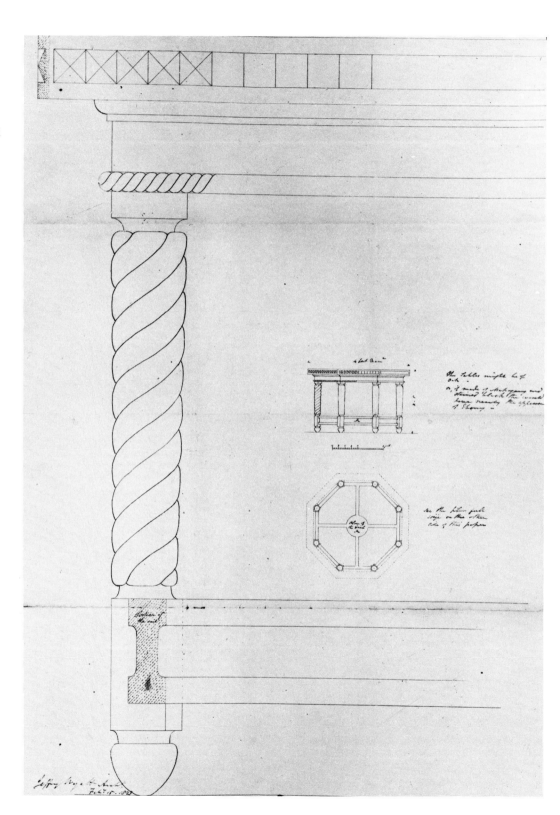

27

Anthony Salvin (1799-1881)

28. Designs for a billiards settle for the hall and a table for the upper gallery, Mamhead, Devonshire for Sir Robert Newman, Bt, *c.* 1838. Sepia pen (265 x 215) table *h.* 2ft 8ins *w.* 2ft 2ins *l.* 4ft 9ins.

Mamhead was Salvin's first major commission (he received it in 1826) and it established his reputation as the leading architect for large country houses in the 'revived domestic Gothic' or Tudor style. The house, with its classically symmetrical plan, was designed in a Tudor style though the stair and ground floor gallery have Perpendicular fan vaulting. Salvin designed the furniture (made on the estate from local holm oak) in a Tudor-Elizabethan style that incorporates Jacobean and Stuart elements. The sketch designs shown here must have been among the last of the drawings he made during the dozen years he worked on Mamhead. Salvin's *Sketch for a high seat for the Hall* seems to have been done with reluctance since he adds *if such a thing is absolutely necessary*. The purpose of the bench is explained by the entrance hall serving also as a billiard room, something Salvin favoured and proposed elsewhere. The settle, raised on a platform, allowed for a good view of the game. The strapwork-like details of the supports to the platform become more elaborate in the supports for a *Table for the Recess in the upper Gallery*. The 80 foot long gallery was designed to display a set of Brussels tapestries and a table, similar to the design shown here, is there still.

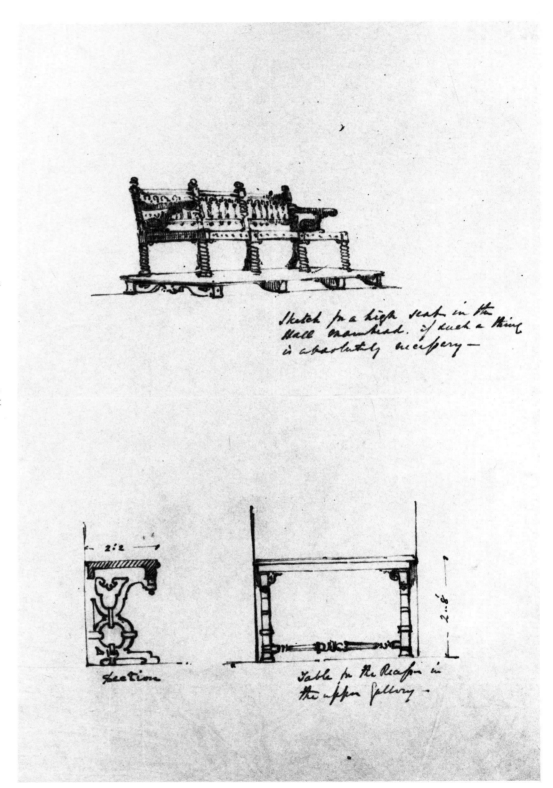

John Buonarotti Papworth (1775-1847)

29. Designs for furniture for Frederick Cass, Little
Grove, East Barnet, Hertfordshire (now Barnet,
London), 1829. Sepia pen and wash with some
pencil and red pen (385 x 320) *scale:* 1in to 1ft and
full size Couch *h.* 2ft 9ins *w.* 2ft *l.* 6ft 6ins, wash-hand-
stand *h.* 2ft 8ins *diam.* 1ft 7ins, towel rail *h.* 3ft 4ins
w. 2ft.

30. Design for a bed for the same client, 1829. Sepia
pen and wash (260 x 525) *scale:* ¾in to 1ft *h.* 10ft
w. 5ft 9ins *l.* 6ft 8ins.

31. Design for the dining room, Little Grove, 1829.
Black and red pen with sepia and blue washes
(465 x 470) *scale:* ¾in to 1ft Room 18ft 6ins x 28ft 6ins.

32. Design for a portfolio stand for James Morrison
MP, Balham Hill House, Wandsworth, London,
c. 1828. Pen with brown, pink and yellow washes
(325 x 200) *scale:* 2ins to 1ft *h.* 3ft 9ins *w.* 3ft *d.* 2ft *see*
Plate VII, p.31.

Papworth, with his flair, versatility and practicality,
must have been the ideal architect for a man with a
substantial mansion and a 94 acre estate bent upon
improving his property and providing comfort and
convenience for his family and servants. Over a
period of nearly twenty years Papworth designed
first the alterations and additions to the house
(which was demolished in 1932), its interior and
fittings, and then attended to the design of the
grounds. A lodge, farm buildings, conservatory and
various horticultural and garden buildings were
added, and palings, vermin grates for drains, an
ironing board, a closet for the children's clogs and
garden shoes were detailed with the same care as the
designs for flowerbeds, chandeliers and furniture.

Papworth's furniture designs for Mr Cass are
eclectic in style though contemporaries would have
described them as 'Grecian or modern'. What the
couch, easy chair (intended for the breakfast room),
wash-hand-stand and towel rail (fig. 29) reveal is the
subordination of 'style' to comfort, ease and
substance, qualities that were to characterise early
Victorian furniture. The mahogany couch was
presumably intended for the principal bedroom
since it shares the same rosette motif and bulbous
legs as the French bed (fig. 30). This, with its buff
and rose hangings trimmed with rose coloured braid
and tassels, is a wonderfully bravura exercise in the
Empire style overlaid by the contemporary tendency
towards massive proportions and eclectic detail. The
more humble basin-stand, with its marble top and
columnar legs, was to be japanned, a method of
painting with 'grounds of opaque colours in
varnish'[11] that was very fashionable at this time.
Papworth had a particular interest in applied finishes
to furniture and a design for a hat and glove stand

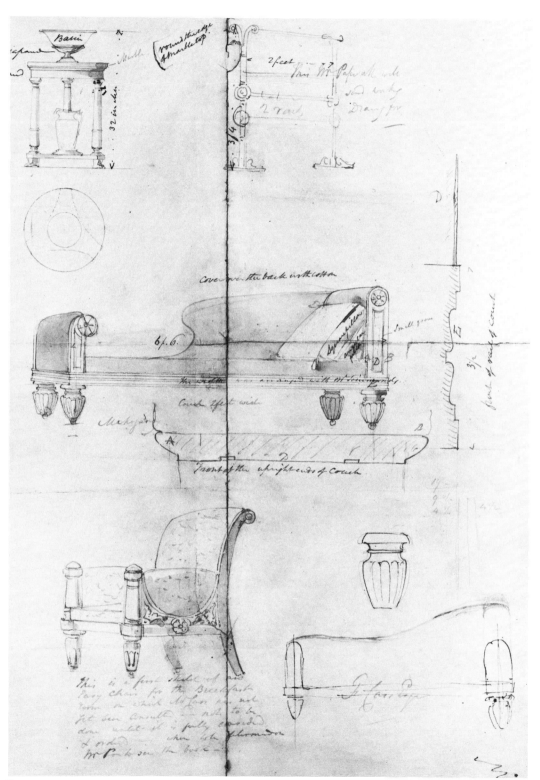

29

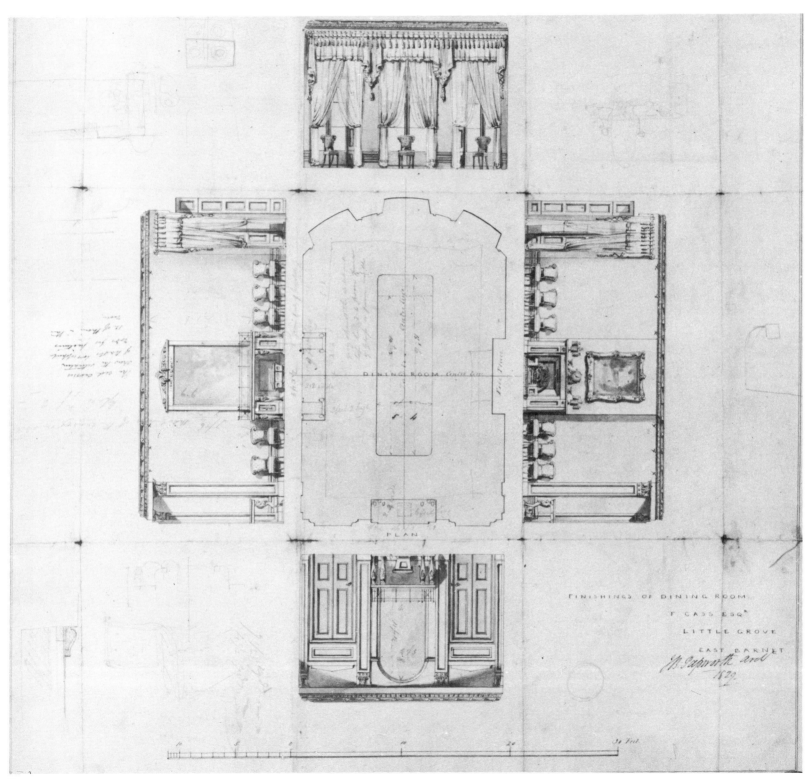

FINISHINGS OF DINING ROOM.
F. CASS ESQ.
LITTLE GROVE
EAST BARNET

for the Cass household has the instruction 'paint . . . in oil in imitation of oak and pollarded oak'. That was not the only false thing about the stand for though it looked like a chest of drawers in fact it was a shelved cupboard with flaps worked by chain pulleys and weights.

For Mr Cass's dining room, Papworth designed all the finishings (fig. 31). For the pilasters he invented a capital with Tudor roses and provided a table extensible to 16ft 6ins, fourteen upholstered chairs arranged in a rather *demodé* way against the wall, sideboards, cellarets, looking-glasses, rods for the pictures to hang from and elaborately draped curtains. Whether the scheme was executed to this design is not known but in 1831, Papworth made another design for a sideboard for Mr Cass different to those shown in the wall-elevations and, most interestingly, it included gas lights.

William Morrison, a draper who made a fortune in a business conducted on the principle of 'small profits and quick returns' bought Balham Hill House in about 1822 (it was demolished in the late 19th century) and employed Papworth to lay out the grounds and to make alterations to the house. Morrison collected books, 'high class . . . paintings' and prints. And it was for his Daniell aquatints of *Oriental Scenery*, bought for £210, and his *Vatican*

Plates that Papworth designed several versions of a portfolio stand. Which of the designs Morrison chose is not known[12] but as well as the more usual double-easel type of folio stand there was a low kneehole cupboard, another low cupboard with floor rollers for the folios to run on and a more elaborate version of the one illustrated standing on a cupboard base with hinged leaves. In the design shown here, Papworth does not make the usual provision for hinged, let-down sides on which the prints could be placed and examined. The folios were withdrawn from the ends and the front is fixed. The design shows both Papworth's fondness for Frenchified detail and the increasing tendency towards heaviness in form and in details of furniture of this period. The paw foot with acanthus decoration is a Neo-Classical motif but has an overscaled vigour that is striking. There is a prophetically Victorian quality about the portfolio stand with its rotundly moulded frieze, rounded 'table' legs and robust construction.

30

Sir Charles Barry (1795-1860)

Designs for furniture for the Reform Club, Pall Mall, London, 1840. Sepia pen (275 x 380, 270 x 375, 275 x 380).

33. Sofa *scale*: ⅜in to 1ft *h*. 3ft *w*. 7ft 9ins.

34. Circular stand *scale*: 1in to 1ft *h*. 2ft 4ins *diam*. 2ft.

35. Occasional table *scale*: ¾in to 1ft *h*. 2ft 4½ins *w*. 3ft *l*. 8ft.

Barry's design for the Reform Club (the winner in a limited competition) was in a Roman High Renaissance style. The grave but gorgeous decoration of its interior, fittings and furniture was carried out in the same neo-Cinquecento manner.

In the drawing room twelve white marble and scagliola Corinthian columns divided the 117 foot long room into three compartments, each of them with a cut-glas chandelier that lit the elaborate gold ornament of the ceiling and was reflected in the large mirrors at either end. These were draped with the golden brown velvet that was used for the curtains, and for the four maplewood sofas which, with the circular maplewood stands, and other furniture, were designed for the room and exist still. The overall effect, enhanced by the gold and silver satin damask that covered the walls, was warmly golden in tone and consistently rich in detail. Barry was among the first to exploit the Italian *palazzo* style and its decorative possibilities. Not an innovative furniture designer, he took established forms and through a sensitive application of ornamental detail and choice of materials secured the aesthetic and stylistic unity that he sought.

The private drawing room had a deeply coved, richly moulded ceiling that was painted in gold and shades of blue. The walls were hung with blue silk damask, the curtains were of blue Utrecht velvet and the furniture, including the tables, was of maplewood with purple wood mouldings. Barry's design for occasional tables was modified in execution: the drawers to the tables were omitted as were the scroll supports shown on the end elevation, and maplewood veneer, not morocco leather, was used for the tops.

In 1853 Barry turned the drawing room into a library, designing the new fittings and retaining much of the original furniture. In 1878 it was redecorated by his son, E.M. Barry, in a polychromatic scheme of gold, bronze, russet brown, crimson and green. The private drawing room became the card room in 1878 and was painted in dark brown, bronze and gold — a colour scheme that has recently been restored. Of all London's West End club-houses, the Reform has remained the least changed, pickled in an atmosphere of ripe stilton, brandy and cigar smoke.

33

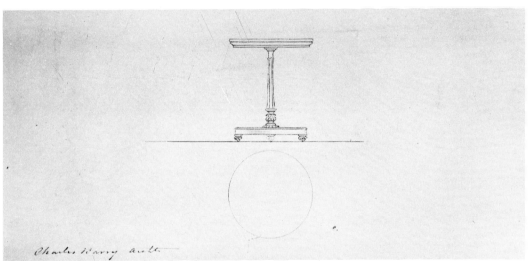

34

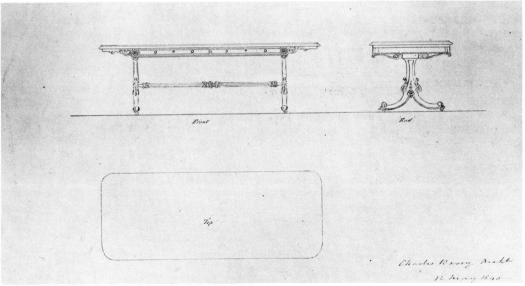

35

Augustus Welby Northmore Pugin (1812-1852)

36. & 37. Designs for side-tables, *c.* 1830. Blue pen (100 x 155, 90 x 185).

38. Design for a side-table, *c.* 1834. Pen with red pen inscriptions (230 x 185) *scale*: ⅜in to 1ft *h.* 3ft *w.* 2ft *l.* 5ft 6ins.

39. Design for the kitchen at Scarisbrick Hall, Lancashire for Charles Scarisbrick (not as executed), 1837. Pencil (310 x 260, top cut to semicircular shape).

40. Design for an octagonal table for the Prince's Gallery at the House of Lords, Palace of Westminster, London *c.* 1846. Pen on tracing paper (355 x 510 mounted in an album) *scale*: 1in to 1ft, 3ins to 1ft and full size *h.* 2ft 7½ins *w.* 6ft.

Pugin's career as a furniture designer was launched in 1827 (when he was only fifteen years old) by a commission 'to design and make working drawings for the Gothic furniture of Windsor Castle'.[13] The side-tables shown here (figs. 36 & 37) are rather similar to those that Pugin designed for Windsor. But these designs, together with others in the Collection, were probably intended as a catalogue for a business 'in the carving and joining line' that he set up in a loft in Hart Street (now Floral Street), Covent Garden, London. Unhappily, it failed within two years because 'in my endeavour to render my designs as handsome as possible I have never spared my money in their execution and as in most cases my prime cost has exceeded my estimate and in no work in which I have hitherto engaged I have been able to clear my remuneration for my exertions I have at length determined to relinquish the *execution* of work myself altogether and to confine myself to my original profession of an architect and designer'.[14]

Pugin, who had learnt his draughtsmanship under the careful tuition of his father, now began to fit himself for a career in architecture by an intensive study of medieval buildings. His first architectural designs were elaborate imaginary schemes and he must soon have realised that employment was more likely to come in the field where he was already known. In 1834 or 1835 he prepared some examples of his furniture designs which, it seems, he presented to Charles Barry with immediate success. One of these, a design for a side-table (fig. 38) shows how far he had moved away from the Regency Gothick 'enormities' of his earlier work. Apart from the complex mouldings of the slab ends there is little enrichment and while the quadrant brace over a central stretcher lacks the bone-like inevitability of later work, it marks a significant stage in Pugin's designs for furniture.

In 1837 Pugin received his first major

36

37

architectural commission: the remodelling of Scarisbrick Hall in Lancashire. Additions to what seems to have been a substantial, 16th century, half-timbered mansion included a new kitchen. Pugin's perspective (fig. 39) clearly shows the relationship between his medievally derived roof structure and the supports for the large working table — particularly in the curvilinear bracing. In *True Principles*[15] he wrote that 'in ancient timber houses . . . we do not find a single feature introduced beyond the decoration of what was necessary for their substantial construction' and that 'the principal tie-beams, rafters, purloins [sic], and braces . . . are

very ornamental' and should not be concealed. This idea of 'honest' or revealed construction was applied in Pugin's kitchen design to the table with its pegged joints as well as to the architecture. The design also reflects his notion of 'propriety' in which 'station and dignity' are here reflected in the scale, form, detailing and ornament. Pugin's designs for the internal decoration and furniture of the Palace of Westminster (fig. 40) reveal his subtle modulation of these elements in conferring degrees of distinction to rooms used by the whole hierarchy of the British parliamentary system, its officers and servants.

More than one hundred types of table were

designed by Pugin for the Houses of Parliament including two octagonal tables for the Prince's Chamber, which is the lobby to the Royal Gallery and one of the grandly furnished State Rooms. The top of the octagonal table was closely framed for strength and the system of legs and supports ensured great stability. Holding to his principle 'that all ornament should consist of enrichment of the essential construction' Pugin placed four fire-breathing dragons (presumably Welsh ones) at the foot of each cross-member, decorated the uprights with a scaly pattern of imbrication and emphasised the ogival supports with a Tudor rose ornament and a leafy crocket. Other tables of the same shape and of similar size in the Palace were plainer.

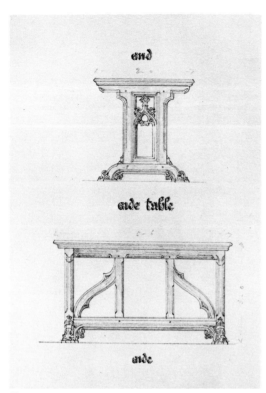

end

side table

side

38

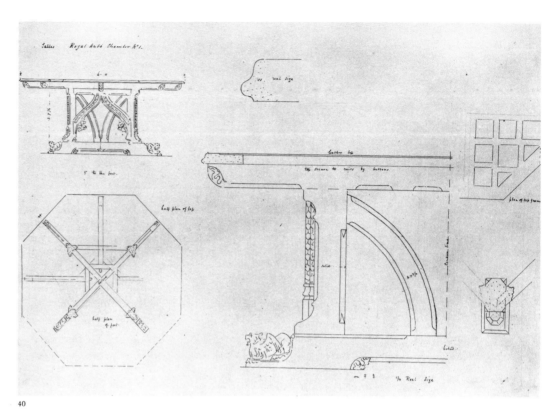

40

James Trubshaw (1777-1853)

41. & 42. Designs for garden seats for Lilleshall Hall, Shropshire, for Elizabeth, Duchess of Sutherland *c.* 1836-9. Pencil (300 x 240), pen (270 x 350).

43. Design for a portfolio stand, 1842. Pen with brown and blue washes (370 x 275) *scale*: 1½ins to 1ft *h.* 3ft 9ins *w.* 3ft 3ins.

Trubshaw thought of himself as a builder and engineer, often signing his drawings *CE* for Civil Engineer and always 'as far as possible avoided . . . interfering with the Professional Architect'. Nevertheless he designed a number of buildings, most of them churches in the Gothic style, including Ketley church for the 2nd of Duke of Sutherland, 1836-9. It was perhaps at about this time that he designed garden seats for Lilleshall Hall for Elizabeth, Duchess of Sutherland (died 1839). Completed in 1833, the house was designed by Sir Jeffry Wyatville who also planned the spacious pleasure grounds. To the south of the house were formal gardens bounded by straight gravel paths and to the north, walks that wound through plantations and over grassy slopes. The 28 acres of gardens were divided from the park by a 'dwarf wall and Hah! Ha!'.[16]

Trubshaw made several designs for garden seats. Probably he felt that the 'old Bowling Green', the rose garden, the circular garden planted with espalier fruit trees and reached by a 750 foot long covered walk of apple trees of many varieties trained over pergolas, the 'open views into the woods' — all suggested seats different in character. Thus he produced two Neo-Classical designs, one in the Elizabethan style, two throne-like Gothic designs as well as the simpler pew-like designs shown here (figs. 41 & 42). Even these are more elaborate than anything suggested by Wyatville's plain Tudor building. They were to be executed in wood, the other designs in stone. But regardless of material every design seems to have been conceived in terms of carved stone. The clue to this may lie in Trubshaw's early training as a mason in his father's yard.

The primitive, hewn qualities of Trubshaw's garden furniture are exhilarating but his detailing, it must be said, was illogical. The bench back and seat have stonework-type mouldings and there is no indication of how they could be attached to the unframed sides. The chair's sides, like slices of rudely shaped tree trunks, are fixed by massive pegs. This kind of revealed construction was illustrated by A.W.N. Pugin in *Gothic Furniture*, a book of designs published in 1835. The use by Trubshaw of revealed carpentry details may be dependent upon Pugin's theory or it may be coincidental. In any case, the combination of carpentry and masonry details in a single *oak chair* is certainly curious.

41

42

43

Trubshaw came from a family long established in Staffordshire as master masons, quarry owners, master builders, sculptors and architects. His eldest son Thomas was an architect and landscape gardener of 'considerable promise'[17] and his early death in 1842 may explain this design (fig. 43) by his father for a portfolio stand. The overall carved decoration, reminiscent of an Elizabethan cartouche, consists of a large, scrolly *T* and reversed *T* with, in the centre, a cross and below this the date *1842*.

A touching memorial, if such it was, to Trubshaw's son and very fitting that it should take the form of a piece specifically described to hold drawings — in this case, presumably those of Thomas Trubshaw.

Sydney Smirke (1799-1877)

44. Design for a bookcase for the library, Luton Hoo, Bedfordshire for John Shaw Leigh, 1849. Pen with grey, buff and brown washes (345 x 495) *scale:* ¾in to 1ft *h.* 10ft 1½ins *w.* 10ft 3ins *d.* 1ft 9ins *see* Plate VIII, p.44.

Luton Hoo, designed by Robert Adam, was ravaged twice by fire: in 1777 and again in 1843. Soon after the second fire, the Marquess of Bute sold the shell to John Shaw Leigh, a Liverpool solicitor who had made a fortune in land and speculation. Sydney Smirke was called in to renovate a house that had earlier been remodelled by his brother Sir Robert Smirke. The Adam library survived the first conflagration but was sufficiently damaged in the fire of 1843 as to require new fittings. Smirke's glazed bookcase was designed in the Italianate style that had superseded the restrained Greek Revivalism acquired from his brother. The pediment, supported on brackets enriched by lion masks and drops, contains the head of Apollo and the panelled doors are ornamented with Renaissance arabesques. The bookcase has not survived. In 1880, the 144 foot long library was turned into a suite of drawing rooms and in 1903 became a ballroom. It is now part of the family wing not open to the public.

44   45

Charles James Richardson (1806-1871)

45a & b. Designs for two cabinets *c.* 1850-60. Pencil (460 x 260, 440 x 270).

Cabinets are traditionally virtuoso exercises in decoration and craftsmanship — receptacles for small, rare and curious objects that delight the owner and astonish visitors. By the 1850s and 1860s, highly elaborate cabinets such as Richardson's, were likely to be exhibition pieces for, say, the Paris International Exhibition of 1855 or the London International Exhibition of 1862. One of Richardson's sketch designs is in what he might have termed 'the French style' but is, more accurately, in his 'floral' style. He was particularly fond of the basket-and-flowers motif found on Louis XIV (and other) furniture and used it freely. His acquaintance with Elizabethan and Jacobean architecture and decoration was more securely based since he published and exhibited numerous highly-wrought and coloured drawings of monuments of that period. Here, the scrolls and swags of the pediment are indebted to Stuart ornament.

In the 1851 Great Exhibition, Richardson showed a number of designs for furniture and decoration as well as an ornately carved oak table and stool in the Elizabethan style. His cabinet designs may have been made with an exhibition in mind or merely, as he wrote of another unexecuted design, 'as a matter of amusement, without any thought that the ideas would ever be carried out'.[18]

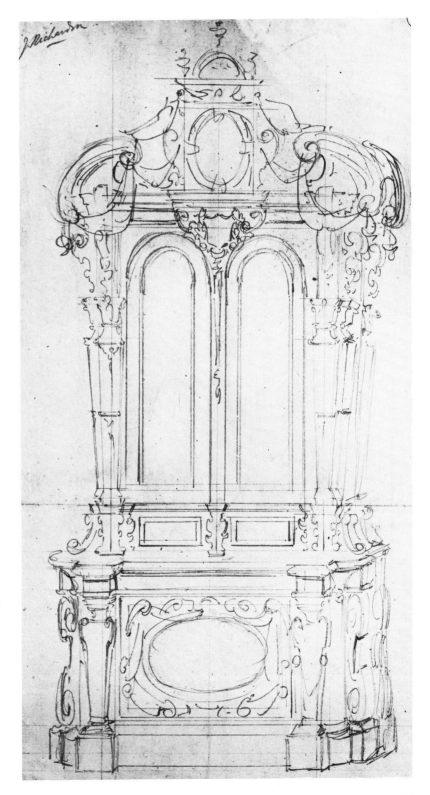

Sir George Gilbert Scott (1811-1878)

46. Design for a table for the music hall at Kelham Hall, Nottinghamshire for John Henry Manners Sutton, *c.* 1861. Pencil with brown and green washes, some pen (860 x 353) *scale*: full size *h.* 2ft 6¼ins *w.* 3ft 2ins *l.* 5ft 6ins *see* Plate IX, p.57.

Kelham Hall, rebuilt after a fire of 1857, is probably Scott's finest country house. He received the commission at about the same time that he published *Remarks on Secular and Domestic Architecture* (1857) and it gave him a chance to show that the Gothic style of architecture could adapt itself to every 'circumstance, position and material' and need not be kept only for churches and public buildings.

Scott favoured 'Early Middle Pointed' Gothic 'invigorated' by features from earlier or later styles. Though loyal on the whole to English Gothic, by the 1850s he had succumbed to fashion and introduced those Italian and French elements apparent at Kelham. The interior was more successful than the exterior and the grandest of the rooms was the music hall. A double-height room with a vaulted ceiling, it has a triforium gallery over an arcade and a huge hooded chimneypiece. A 19th century photograph shows it furnished with over-stuffed sofas and armchairs but the splendid table especially designed for the room does not appear. It is not at Kelham now and perhaps was never executed. Certainly Scott's vision of the country house proprietor as 'blessed with wealth' was not true of John Henry Manners Sutton, local MP and landowner. For though he had a very decent income 'ambition led him to exceed what [was] proportioned to the means placed by Providence in his hands'. At some stage funds ran out and it is likely that the table, along with the second staircase, the conservatory and much internal decoration, was dispensed with.

The table was to have been executed in bog oak with the frieze rail and end stretchers made from lighter toned wainscot oak and the top inlaid in geometric patterns that echo those of the floor. The carved details are derived, in the main, from 12th and 13th century English Gothic stonework and the roundel with shield, the leafy capital and cabbage-like rose are also found on the chimneypiece of the music hall. It is unlikely that Scott was closely concerned with the design of the table for he was now at the height of his career and relied heavily on the twenty seven or so assistants and pupils in his office. Of the hundreds of surviving drawings for Kelham Hall, only a *rough section* is in Scott's hand. The others are by Arthur Baker and Joseph and Jabez Bignell.[19] In a practice where 'nearly five hundred churches [and] thirty-nine cathedrals . . . were built or interfered with' Scott's staff were well used to producing working drawings for pulpits, bishops's thrones, pews and so on. But designs for domestic or secular furniture were rarely prepared and this makes even more interesting the design shown here.

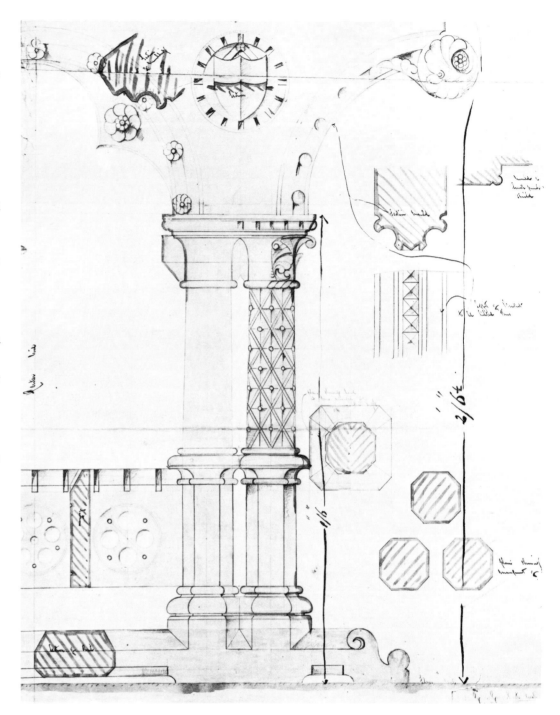

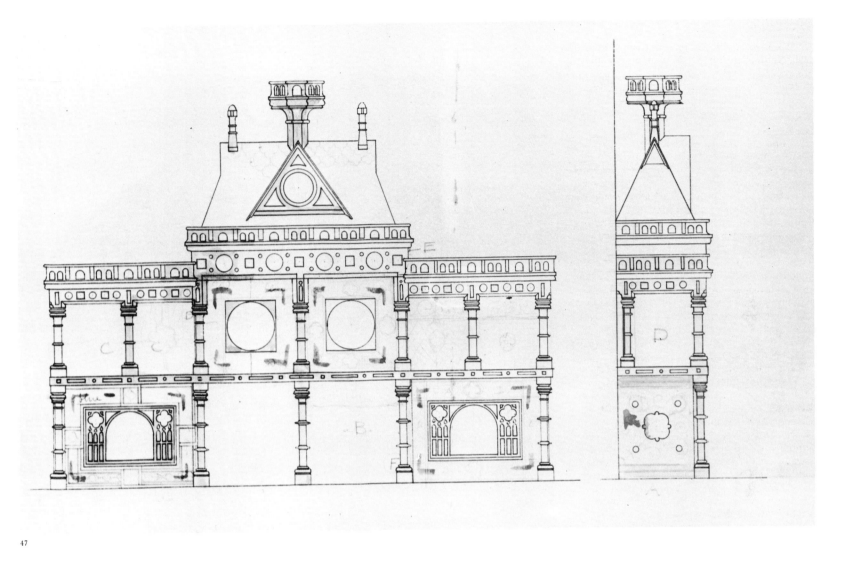

47

William Burges (1827-1881)

Designs for furniture for the architect's own use, at 15 Buckingham Street and the Tower House, Melbury Road, London, 1869-80.

47. & 48. Design for the Dog Cabinet, 1869. Elevation (probably a record drawing). Pen and coloured washes with some pencil (280 x 450) *scale*: 2ins to 1ft. Detail of decoration of lower doors. Pencil and coloured washes (355 x 510) *scale*: full size *h*. 3ft 10½ins *w*. 5ft *d*. 11½ins *see* Plate X, p.58.

49. Design for the Peacock Cabinet, 1873. Pencil and black wash on detail paper (1180 x 420) *scale*: full size *h*. 3ft 3½ ins *w*. 2ft 4ins *d*. 1ft 0½in.

50. Design for a sideboard, partly re-using existing pieces, 1875. Pencil and coloured washes (530 x 665) *scale*: 2ins to 1ft *h*. 7ft 3ins *w*. 5ft *d*. 1ft 11¼ins *see* Plate XI, p.59.

51. Design for a drawing table, 1876. Pen with yellow, brown and grey washes, some pencil (320 x 535) *scale*: 1½ins to 1ft *h*. 2ft 4ins and 3ft 0½in *w*. 4ft 6ins *d*. 2ft 8ins.

52. & 53. Designs for a table, dressing table and wash-hand-stand to be executed in bronze, 1880. Pen with green and brown washes (350 x 510, 330 x 530) *scale*: 1in to 1ft and full size *w*. 2ft 10ins all *d*. 1ft 10ins, table *h*. 2ft 4ins, dressing table *h*. 4ft 4ins, wash-hand-stand *h*. 3ft 6½ins.

48

William Burges was the first of the 19th century furniture designers to explore the medieval precedents for painted furniture and both inventiveness and humour were expressed in the often elaborate iconography that was devised for beds, cabinets, bookcases, wardrobes and other pieces. Each of Burges's designs for furniture was designed for a particular function in a particular room for a particular client — often himself.

In June 1865 Burges moved into chambers at 15 Buckingham Street, London. This pleasant terrace overlooking the river was built in the late 17th century and over the next twenty years, Burges's aggressively medievalist decoration swallowed up the classical interiors — a contrast that must have been striking.

The Dog Cabinet (figs. 47 & 48) was designed to go over the fireplace in Burges's office. Later it was put in the 'day nursery' (jokingly called thus by Burges who was, in fact, a bachelor) at the Tower House. Photographs of the cabinet at Buckingham Street (in an album at the RIBA.[20]) show it laden with artistic bric-a-brac on a fringed mantelshelf beneath a wall hung with pieces of armour. The photographs also show that the cabinet was decorated (by Charles Rossiter) with portraits of Burges's dogs. On the four doors were a poodle called Pinkie, who was also immortalised in the mosaic floor of the Tower House front porch, and sealyhams Tiger, Dandie and Bogie with, in the small roundels of the gallery, portraits of Bogie's puppies: Snob, Yokel, Swell and Curate. The rest of the painted decoration, in keeping with Burges's principle that painting should 'judiciously alternate with ornament'[21] consists of diaper patterns painted in red, blue and green with the main structure gilded. The gabled roof was probably derived from the late 13th century *armoire* once in Noyon Cathedral. The doors, windows and colonettes below add to the doll's house-like quality of the cabinet. and it did indeed end up, battered to death, in a real nursery.

For his bedroom at Buckingham Street, Burges designed the Peacock Cabinet, called thus because of the peacock's tail decoration of the back board (fig. 49). Also for his bedroom he designed the Sleeping Beauty Bed, Narcissus Wash-hand-stand, Crocker Dressing table and a chest of drawers painted with joky references to its contents. All of these were later put in Burges's bedroom at the Tower House except for the cabinet which was placed in the drawing room.

Burges had a number of hanging cabinets and shelves, each of an individual design, that were placed over chimneypieces, chests of drawers, wash-hand-stands and in corners. They were designed to hold the growing collection of pots, caskets, enamels, bronzes and other treasures that filled his

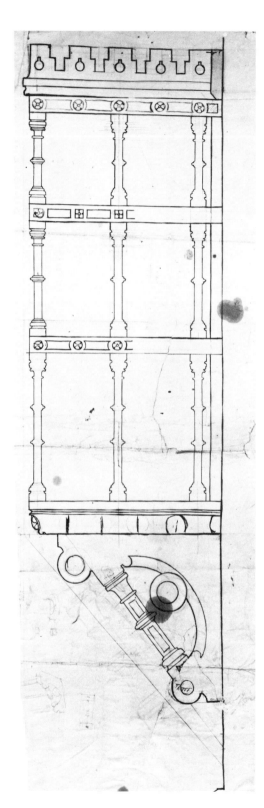

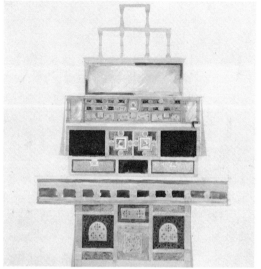

50

'Aladdin's Palace'. The Peacock Cabinet was made of oak and gilded. The back board was decorated with an inlay, probably of mother of pearl, and the edges of the shelves had rectangular sunk panels containing richly coloured marbles and semi-precious stones. The overall design is, for Burges, light, open and almost graceful though the brackets are reassuringly tough. In his later furniture Burges did move away from the 'elephantine influence . . . [of] his early work'[22] towards a lighter handling, using more accomplished craftsmen and relying less on 'plank Gothic' and anecdotal decoration.

In March 1878, Burges moved to the dream house he had built for himself in Melbury Road. He had begun work on the design of the Tower House on 13 July 1875 and from that date designs for his own furniture must have been made mindful of their new setting. The dining room of the Tower House was less strongly thematic than the other rooms. The wall decorations are said to have been suggested by Chaucer's 'House of Fame'. Above the dark marble dado marched what seems like the cast list from a monster Christmas pantomine: Jack and the Beanstalk, Sleeping Beauty, Little Red Riding Hood, Ali Baba and the Forty Thieves, the Babes in the Wood, Cinderella, Aladdin and so on. The furniture included a glass-fronted cabinet from Buckingham Street, the Conditions of Life escritoire made in 1867, two walnut sideboards made early in 1877 and another sideboard that seems to have been made partly from existing units (fig. 50). All were stuffed with 'choice specimens of dining-table silver and service'[23] and with 'cups of jade . . . goblets of silver and rock-crystal set with gems and quaint work . . . precious drinking vessels which those who have had the privilege of dining with Mr Burges know the

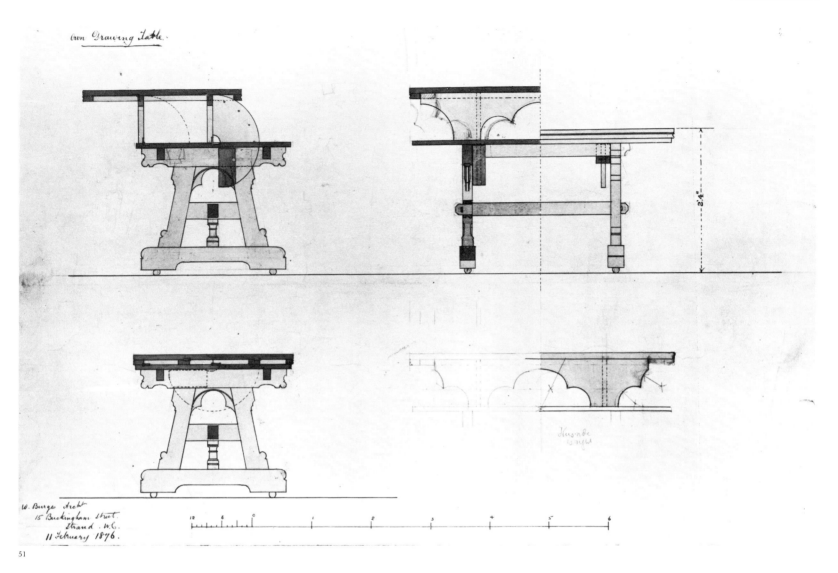

Iron Drawing Table.

W. Burges Archt
15 Buckingham Street
Strand . W.C.
11 February 1876.

51

pleasure (and pain) of handling'.[24] Virtually everything in the Tower House 'from the furniture down to the utensils and knives and forks'[25] was designed by Burges.

The nine-stage sideboard shown here (fig. 50) was plain in form but richly decorated. Burges's estimate book[26] shows that in October 1875 Walden (a joiner frequently employed by Burges) estimated £20 for the sideboard including 10 shillings for 'three new drawers'. He later made 'three pierced and carved panels' and provided 'sundry key plates'. T. Nicholls did the intricate carving including six leaves and three mice on the wide drawers in the centre and C. Campbell executed the painted decoration. The total cost was about £67 excluding the inserts of malachite, lapis lazuli and cornelian that provided

an added brilliance.

It seems likely that the drawing table shown here (fig. 51) was designed for Burges's old chambers in Buckingham Street, retained as his office when he moved to the Tower House. Artists' or architects' tables with hinged slopes, extending leaves and swing drawers were introduced early in the 18th century. They were elegant, mahogany pieces that concealed their function and were intended for the drawing room (or library) rather than the drawing office. More practical was the use of a drawing board (either flat or propped on a convenient book) on a sturdy table. Improved drawing boards with battens to prevent warping were in use by the beginning of the 19th century and from the 1850s a number of patents were taken out for drawing tables that either

continued the polite parlour vein of earlier models or tended towards the over-ingenious.

Burges made two designs, at least, for drawing tables for his own use. His requirements were for a table that could be adjusted to sitting or standing height and on which an antiquarian board could be used. Thus the double-rising tops are 55½ x 32½ inches in size and right-angled hinges and a regulator with pins provide alternative drawing positions. The supports are massive and while the stretcher is fixed by an emphatic joinery detail, the fat early Gothic mouldings are borrowed from stonework.[27] Another, smaller drawing table with an adjustable slope that Burges also designed was probably intended for use at home. An entry in his notebook for February 1878[28] under 'things at

Melbury Road' lists a drawing table and various drawing materials. The need for a drawing table both at home and at work is explained by the immense number of drawings that Burges produced. For though he deliberately restricted the size of his practice, taking on no more than he 'could produce as his own personal design', he had few assistants and, committed to close attention to every detail of construction, decoration and furniture, Burges produced sheet upon sheet of working drawings of great precision. He disliked the 'scribble style' and recommended to students the use of 'strong thick lines'.[29]

Burges was adventurous in his choice and use of materials and, supported by a wide range of specialist craftsmen, he explored the possibilities of new materials and combined traditional ones in new ways. Burges seems to have had an affinity for metal. He collected armour (much of it now in the British Museum) and designed sumptuous ecclesiastical and domestic *orfevrerie*. Early in 1880 he made designs for a three-lobed table that was cast in bronze (fig. 52). It was probably placed in the hall of the Tower House between the bronze-clad front and garden doors. A three-lobed dressing table with a circular bronze mirror together with a matching wash-hand-stand, (fig. 53) designed at the same time, seem not to have been executed. Bronze had been used for furniture, as well as for sculpture and decorative objects, since the Graeco-Roman period and for *bronzes d'ameublement* in 18th and 19th century France. Its use for furniture in this country and at this date was unusual but Burges had considerable experience of bronze-working. For Castell Coch, the Welsh castle rebuilt for Lord Bute from 1872, for example, Burges designed a fountain, doors, flower boxes, statues, candlesticks and a mantelpiece that were all cast in bronze. At the time he designed the trefoil tables Burges was arranging for the casting of the figure of Fame that decorated his dining room chimneypiece. The tables show the designer's consistent fondness for compass-drawn shapes but the attenuated legs and sparseness of ornament are novel. The hall table was probably the last piece of furniture made for Burges's own use for he died in the following year after unwisely going for a 'long drive in a dog cart and [getting] very cold'.[30] Lethaby wrote[31] that 'when the house was finished the hearse was at the door' though, in fact, Burges never did complete the decoration and furnishing of his 'Aladdin's Palace'.

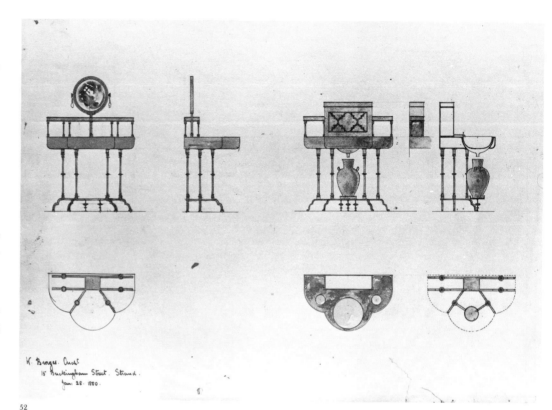

52

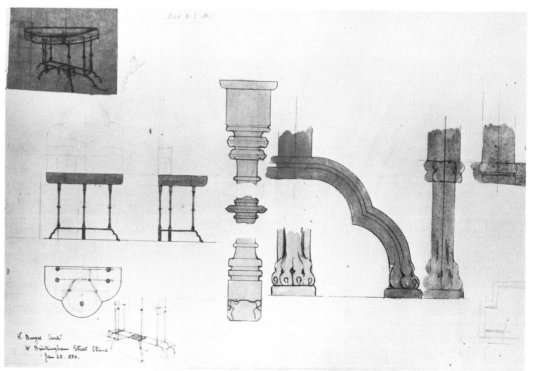

53

54

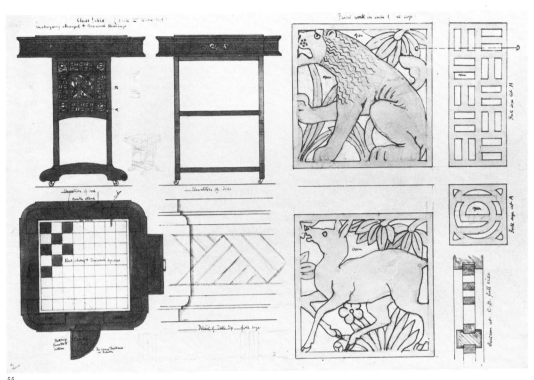

55

Edward William Godwin (1833-1886)

Designs for furniture for Dromore Castle, Country Limerick, Ireland for the 3rd Earl of Limerick, 1869.

54. Sideboard for the dining hall. Sepia pen and wash (230 x 305) *scale*: ½in to 1ft *h*. 10ft 2ins *w*. 14ft 2ins *see* Plate XII, p.60.

55. Chess table. Pen with yellow, grey and brown washes, some pencil (330 x 495) *scale*: 2ins to 1ft and full size *h*. 2ft 5¼ins *w*. 2ft 1in.

56. Drawing room furniture. Pen and coloured washes (325 x 500) *scale*: 1in to 1ft and full size Card table *h*. 2ft 6ins *w*. 1ft 7ins *l*. 3ft 1in, armchair No.1 *h*. 2ft 6ins *w*. 2ft *d*. 2ft 1in, armchair No.2 *h*. 2ft 5ins *w*. 2ft 1in *d*. 2ft 1in, circular settee *h*. 4ft 3ins *diam*. 5ft 10ins, chair *h*. 3ft 2ins *w*. 1ft 6ins *d*. 1ft 7ins, whatnot *h*. 4ft 9ins *w*. 2ft *d*. 1ft 6ins, sofa *h*. 2ft 9ins *w*. 5ft 6ins *d*. 2ft.

57. Eagle chair. Pen with brown and yellow washes, some pencil (detail from a sheet 325 x 500) *scale*: 1in to 1ft and full size *h*. 3ft *w*. 2ft 3ins *d*. 1ft 8ins.

In 1866 Godwin was commissioned by the young Lord Limerick to design a castle on a site near Pallaskenry. Godwin's design for Castle Dromore[32] was (except for the round tower which belonged to an earlier age) an archaeologically correct version of Irish castle architecture of the 15th and 16th centuries. The paraphernalia of medieval defensive warfare: keep, towers, turrets, crenellations, machicolations and battered walls gave a romantic silhouette. But Dromore, unique among 19th century castles, was actually defensible. Designed in the year of the Fenian rising, the architect described how 'the corridors are kept on the outer side of the building and all the entrances are well guarded, so that . . . the inmates . . . might not only feel secure themselves but be able to give shelter to others'.[33]

Inside the castle, Godwin designed the decorations as a unity: furniture, stained glass, metalwork, tiles, carpets and fabrics. But unlike his friend William Burges who in his equally comprehensive scheme for Cardiff Castle (begun two years before) achieved homogeneity through his 'total immersion in a vision of the past',[34] Godwin found stimulus in a variety of sources. His sketchbooks for this period[35] show that he studied English and Welsh as well as Irish castles, made notes and sketches of wall decorations in various medieval churches, and copied details of ornament from illuminated manuscripts in the British Musuem and the Royal Irish Academy. Godwin also drew birds, animals and plants from life and he sketched details from Japanese woodcuts, discovering as he did so congruences in the formalized pattern-making of Western medieval art and Eastern art. Something of all these sources is apparent in his decorations and furniture for Dromore.

The walls of the dining hall at Dromore were to have been washed in a grey-green, with bands of stylized ornament and a frieze of conventionalized sloe trees in blue and white pots alternating with figures depicting such virtues as Industry and Chastity. Painted by Henry Stacy Marks, the decorations were never completed because of problems created by damp. In his design for the buffet-sideboard (fig. 54) Godwin made a concession to the Gothic building by the use of oiled wainscot oak and the occasional Gothic detail. A more or less obligatory coat of arms decorates the gable but it is surmounted by a carved peacock, a favourite motif of the Aesthetic Movement, here apparently used by Godwin for the first time. The sideboard owes something of its simplicity, rectilinearity and balance of solid and void to Godwin's knowledge of Japanese woodwork derived from his study of Japanese prints. These became available in Britain only after the International Exhibition of 1862, in London. Burges and Shaw also collected such prints but Godwin's debt was more profound. For William Burges, the life style and artefacts of the East were the nearest contemporary equivalents to Western medievalism. Norman Shaw and W.E. Nesfield were most interested in the decorative motifs of Japanese applied art while Godwin found inspiration not only in the ornament, delicacy and light, clear colours of

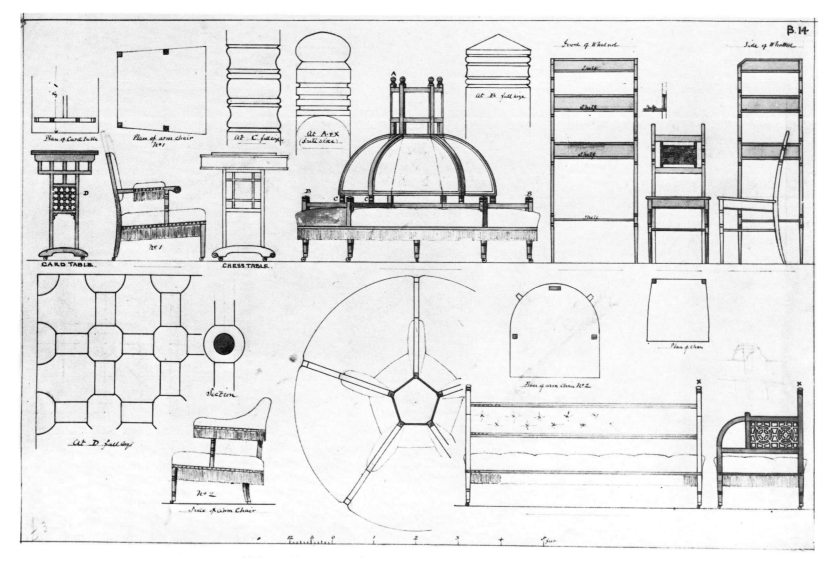

Japanese woodcuts but also in the proportions, structure and details of architectural woodwork that were often revealed. However, even those designs for furniture that he labelled 'Anglo-Japanese' are unlike anything produced in Japan. It was rather that the stimulus of Eastern art allowed him to throw off the yoke of revivalism and encouraged invention.

Godwin's design for a chess table (fig. 55) for Dromore Castle is both stylish and practical. Equipped with drawers and wells for the chess pieces and quadrant candlestands, the chess squares are of *real ebony & boxwood*. The lion and fawn of the ends are borrowed from the Limerick coat of arms and, allowed off their hind legs, have assumed the graceful attitudes found in Chinese papercuts. The chess table (made for £2) was part of a suite of

drawing room furniture (fig. 56) that included two card tables with end panels of Turkish-type lattice work: an idea perhaps borrowed from William Burges.[36] There were also two whatnots, six 'light chairs with plaited fine straw backs', a sofa with pierced ends similar to those of the chess table, two armchairs and a 'circular settee with receptacle for flowers in centre'. The upholstered furniture was covered with 'yellow satin in colour like that known in China as Imperial yellow'. All of the drawing room furniture was made in 'mahogany ebonized by penetrating stain and dry polished' by William Watt's Art Furniture Company. The black and yellow furniture, faintly Eastern in character, was placed in a room colour washed blue and green with a dark boarded ceiling painted with a stylized decoration

based on the interlaced ornament of Celtic manuscripts.[37]

Godwin's eagle chair shows a fascinating mixture of sources. In April 1869, as his sketchbooks[38] show he made several studies of a goshawk's head, noting the 'lemon colour' and 'large black centre' of its eye. The naturalistic detail of the eagle chair reproduces almost exactly this close observation of a goshawk. The stylized wing decoration (pencilled-in) reinforces the notion of reference to the hawk-headed Egyptian gods, Horus and Ra. The rest of this elegant throne for a modern, Aesthetical Irish chieftain is pure invention.

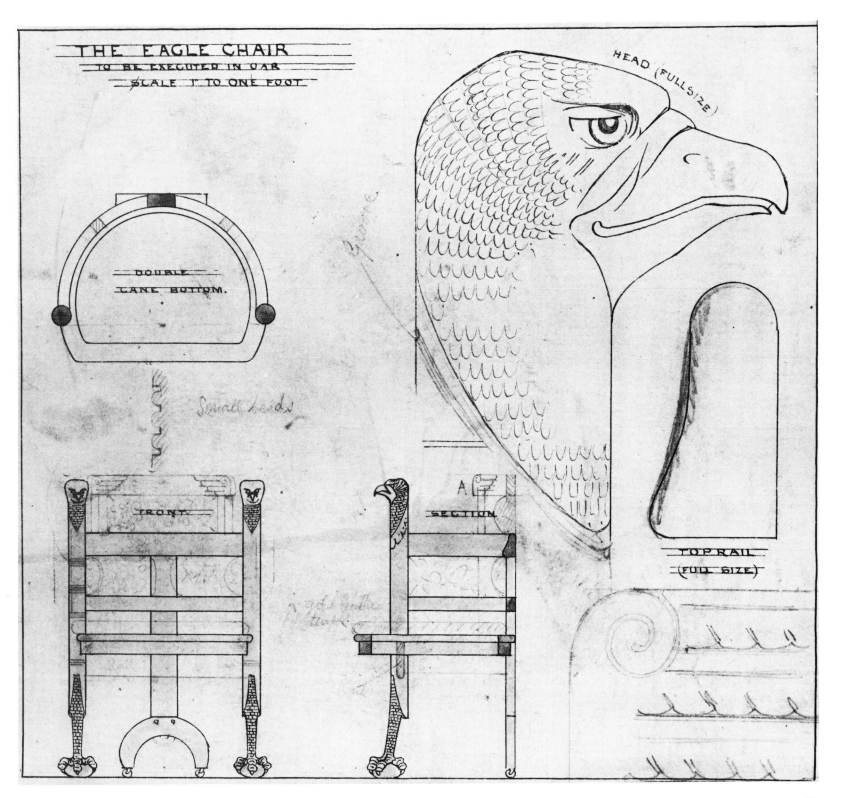

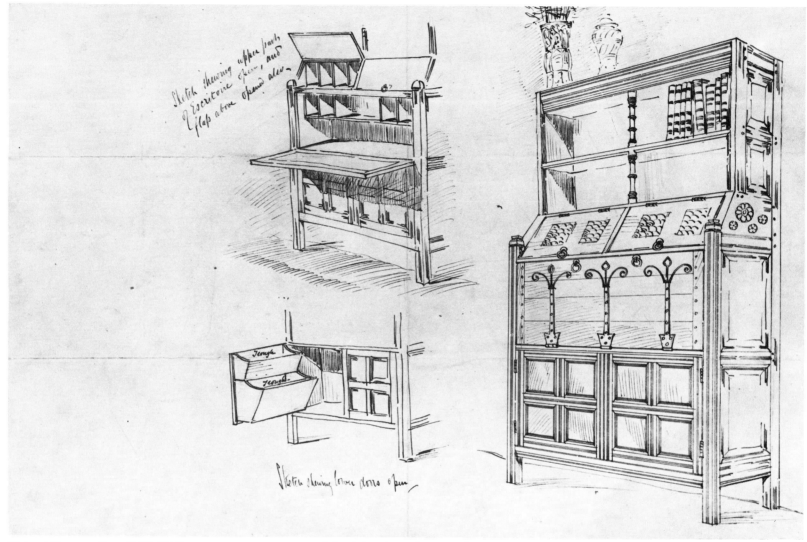

Richard Norman Shaw (1831-1912)

58. Design for a writing table/bookcase, c. 1862-3. Sepia pen (270 x 385).

Shaw's first executed design was a writing table/ bookcase, now in the Victoria and Albert Museum. A virtuoso piece, exhibited at the Architectural Exhibition, 1861 and the London International Exhibition of 1862, it was in the early Gothic style revived by William Burges and others. It received much the same kind of criticism that the earlier essays of others in the medievalist 'dolls' house' style had provoked. A correspondent to *The Builder*[39] wrote that 'the whole structure has the appearance of a miniature stone building which is surely not desirable in furniture of wood'. Shaw must have agreed with this view for he gave the desk/bookcase

away and the design shown here reveals no 'misapplication of stone construction to wood'.

The present design was probably made in 1862 or 1863[40] and may not have been executed. Shaw initially set up in practice from his home in St John's Wood, London but early in 1863 moved to an office that he shared with William Eden Nesfield. They had both been articled to William Burn and had gone on sketching tours together, including a trip to Sussex in September 1862 that was to prove crucial in their invention (based on the vernacular of the Weald) of the Old English style. The sketchbooks of both men for this period[41] have many details that could have furnished the elements of the writing table/bookcase. There are sketches of door hinges of the kind used for the writing flap and the fondness of both for circular ornament shows itself in many

sketches, including one by Shaw of a Jacobean chair that has motifs almost identical to those he uses for the cheeks of the desk/bookcase. The scaley decoration of the sloping lids to the writing table could suggest tile-hanging or pargetting. However, in Nesfield's sketchbook there are details, copied from Japanese prints, of textile designs, one of which is very similar to the decorative motif of the desk. Both Shaw and Nesfield were interested in the Art of Japan and of the Far East. Their choice of decoration often reveals this and so too, do the Nankeen pots on the bookcase — the first perhaps of Shaw's collection of blue and white porcelain. Overall, the cabinet is not exotic. The plain panelling, expressed dowelling, emphatic ironmongery, functional organisation and sturdy form are markedly straightforward, honest and 'Old English'.

Alfred Waterhouse (1830-1905)

Designs for furniture for Manchester Town Hall, c.1877.

59. Detail of table leg. Sepia pen and wash (230 x 160).

60. Settee. Sepia pen and green wash (210 x 225).

61. Chair. Sepia pen and green wash (230 x 170) h. 3ft 2¼ins w. 1ft 7½ins d. 1ft 8½ins.

Waterhouse won the competition for a new Manchester Town Hall in 1868 with a design described in the souvenir book produced to mark the opening of the building in 1877 as 'thirteenth century Gothic suffused with the feeling and spirit of the present age'.[42] Waterhouse, however, saw his design as 'essentially of the nineteenth century' and though he used the town halls of Northern Europe as a model his approach was uninhibited by archaeological correctness and the result was admirably suited to the workaday and ceremonial requirements of a 'municipal palace'.

Besides office furniture, Waterhouse designed a great deal of furniture for the reception rooms and the mayor's private apartments. His earlier furniture had been strongly influenced by Pugin's at the Palace of Westminster and the revealed construction, x-shaped stretchers and gables of some of the pieces designed for Manchester Town Hall reveal this continued dependence. The most individual of Waterhouse's Town Hall furniture is in the Old English style that he probably arrived at through his friendship with Norman Shaw. It is a style that bridges the Reformed Gothic and Aesthetic Movements and Waterhouse used if from the late 1860s well into the 1880s. He used it for furniture but not (except for Blackmoor House) for architecture. And though his use of Old English was extensive, it was not exclusive. He designed for Girton College much lighter furniture that harmonized with the Japanese-type wallpapers and curtains that he selected.

Waterhouse was a pragmatist and his selection of a style was based on functional and associational considerations. Old English style furniture — the embodiment of certain techniques of mechanical woodworking and inherently eclectic, suited Waterhouse. It was versatile and accorded well with a variety of building types designed in Gothic, Romanesque, Tudor or Francois Premier styles and, lending itself to mechanical production, was economical. Details for each of Waterhouse's buildings differ but in a large practice often designing very large buildings, a uniform repetition of ornamental forms devised by the architect and machine-executed, eliminated assistant and craftsman from the design process and ensured

DINING·TABLE·LEGS· in gt. Dining room.

SKETCH·FOR·SETTEE·IN·THE·RECEPTION·ROOM·

the Waterhouse imprint on his productions without recourse to the one-scheme-at-a-time practice of Burges or Webb.

Among the furniture designs for the town hall is a design for an *ordinary chair* (fig. 61) whose ancestry goes back through the traditional turned chair of the 17th century to the Romanesque period. The uprights of the back with round and square sections illustrate the possibilities of lathe technique. The incised rails hold a *stuffed cushion* with a *tooled pattern* based on asymmetrical Japanese floral designs. The mayor's parlour had an entire suite of these chairs and there were variants of this design in some of the reception rooms. Some examples exist still at the town hall though with the city arms in gilt instead of the floral design first proposed.

The settee for the *reception room* (fig. 60) uses lattice work in a way that emphasises the overall grid-like appearance of the piece. Much of Waterhouse's furniture appears to be composed on the basis of a

grid, paralleling the way in which he organised his buildings. Similar latticing is found in Turkish woodwork and Waterhouse may have seen examples when he visited Constantinople as a young man or, as a visitor to William Burges's house where it was used for window screens. Rows of spindle turnings used for the back and arms of the settee are another characteristic Waterhouse device that appear on his designs for chairs, desks, tables, chimneypieces and so on. Though no four-seater settees are now at the town hall, there is a three-seater settee (7 foot long) very similar to the one illustrated here.

Contemporary photographs of the *Gt Dining Room* show three tables, one with eight legs (21 foot long) and two with six legs (11 foot long). These survive still though used in another part of the building. The carved decoration of the legs is similar to the detail illustrated here (fig. 59) though there are small individual differences between each set of legs. A constructional variation was the addition of cusped

brackets to the top of each tbale leg.[43]

Of the twenty one designs for furniture for Manchester town hall at the RIBA most are signed *Doveston, Bird & Hull*, a Manchester furniture manufacturing firm while a few are signed *E. Goodall & Co.* These and other of Waterhouse's designs for furniture have shared the general condemnation of 'his defects of taste' that saddened his last years. Only fairly recently has this opinion been revised. Waterhouse's obituary in the *Building News* deplored in his architecture 'a wiriness of outline, a redundancy of repeated ornament and a want of go and abandon'. A criticism that could be applied to his furniture designs, as might Goodhart-Rendel's more recent judgement of Waterhouse's work as 'definite, logical and brave'.

61

George Aitchison (1825-1910)

62. Design for a sideboard for the dining room at 15 Berkeley Square, London, for Frederick Lehmann 1874. Pen and wash with chinese white and gold paint (505 x 715) *scale:* 2ins to 1ft *h.* 3ft *w.* 7ft 6ins *d.* 3ft.

An important part of Aitchison's career was concerned with the decoration of the town houses of a rich, art-loving and influential clientele. Frederick Lehmann's house in Berkeley Square was considered by some contemporaries to be Aitchison's *chef d'oeuvre*.[44] For each room he devised a distinctive scheme of intricate painted decoration and some of the friezes, for example, were painted by Henry Smallfield and Albert Moore. Moore also collaborated on the design of four ivory plaques depicting hunting, fishing, harvesting and grape gathering that were inlaid on a sideboard designed by Aitchison for the dining room.[45] The architect kept the 18th century dark oak ceiling and pilastered ebony chimneypiece and designed the furniture in a 'corresponding shade'. Aitchison often chose ebony or ebonized woodwork and some of his interior designs show dados, skirtings, doors, chimneypieces and bookcases that are an inky black contrast to the rich, glowing colours of the walls. Though the ebony, incised ornament and decorative plaques of the *serving table* are the hallmarks of Art Furniture, Aitchison's furniture does not share the self-conscious 'artiness' of much Aesthetic Movement design. Intended for the Mayfair dining room of a millionaire, the sideboard has a rich and sober exclusiveness. Its expensive details, including the stylized decoration of the top, and the architectural elements of pilaster, cornice, frieze and plinth were derived from Italian or French Renaissance sources, popularised by Owen Jones's *Grammar of Ornament* (1856).

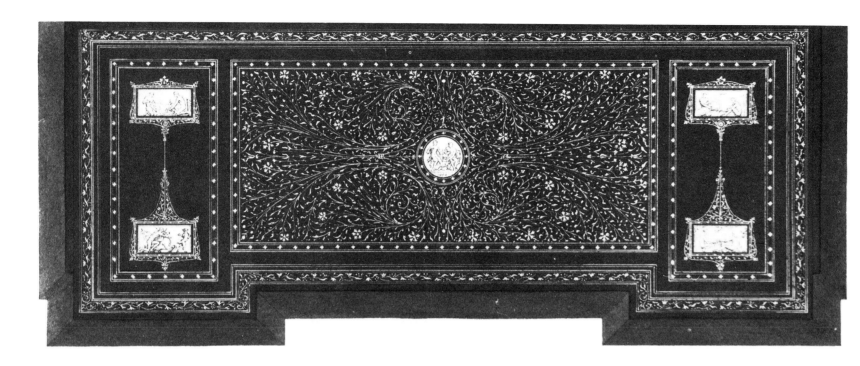

62

Philip Webb (1831-1915)

63. Design for a sideboard, *c.*1870. Pen on tracing paper (380 x 280) *scale:* 1½ins to 1ft and full size *h.* 4ft 9ins *w.* 3ft 5ins *d.* 2ft 1in.

64. Design for the carving of a cabinet and picture frame, *c.* 1880. Sepia pen and wash (495 x 730) *scale:* full size.

65. Design for a movable bookcase for the drawing room of Forthampton Court, Gloucestershire for John Yorke, 1891. Pencil (505 x 755) *scale:* 1in to 1ft *h.* 10ft 9ins *w.* 3ft 7½ins *d.* 3ft 7½ins.

Webb's earliest furniture designs, made in what he called 'my Gothic days', were associated with William Morris and 'the Firm' they set up in 1861. These were massive, primitive pieces joiner-made of oak. Cabinets and wardrobes were given large flat surfaces suitable for representational paintings. The re-organisation of Morris & Co in 1875 coincided, more or less, with a move by Webb away from the somewhat gloomy richness of his early interiors with their heavy pieces of furniture, to white-painted or pale oak panelled interiors that often incorporated fitted furniture: shelves, cupboards, sideboards, benches and the like. While it was possible to buy a Webb-designed sideboard or settle off-the-peg, in his decorative schemes of the '80s and '90s such furniture was tailored to the panelled lining of a room. Cornice, rails, skirting and panels were united with chimneypiece, doors and windows to form a satisfying architectural whole.

Webb's account book[46] shows what his design charges to Morris's firm were: from 5/- for a dressing table, towel rail or decanter, 10/- for a chair, looking-glass or jam dish and cover, £1 for a bookcase, wardrobe or brooch, £2 for an iron bedstead and £2.10/- for a sideboard. Perhaps that last charge refers to the sideboard design shown here (fig. 63) that was to be executed in teak, an unusual choice of material. It was probably designed before 1874 (at which date, the album in which it is mounted, was compiled). A similar sideboard, made of walnut, was illustrated in a Morris & Co catalogue, *c.* 1910 and cost £25. Wider (5ft 2ins, with three drawers) it has the same form and details as the sideboard shown here. Both were derived from the homely, country-made kitchen dresser of the 17th century. In his later work, Webb absorbed something of the serene qualities of Stuart and early Georgian design though he was never at any time a copyist. His belief was in the 'common tradition' and in 'customary ways' and he claimed to be most satisfied with his work when it looked 'commonplace'.

It is not known who was the *FS* that died aged seventeen years and in whose memory Philip Webb designed (fig. 64) *a cabinet to contain a picture and mask*

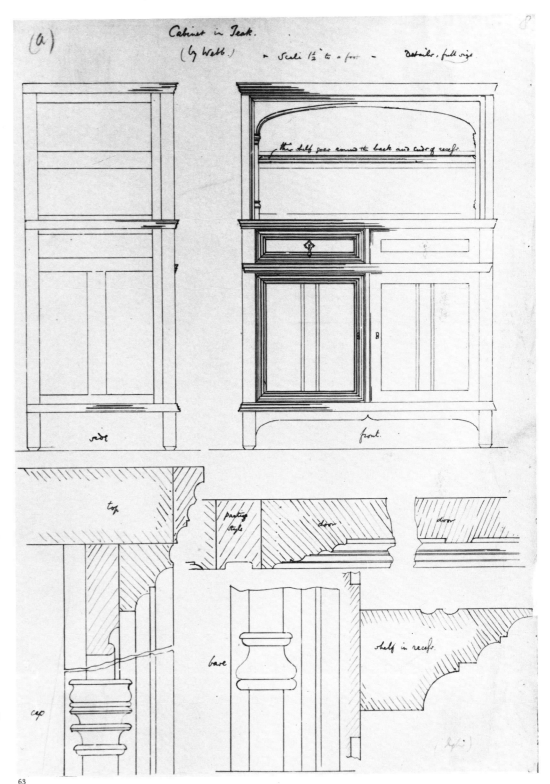

63

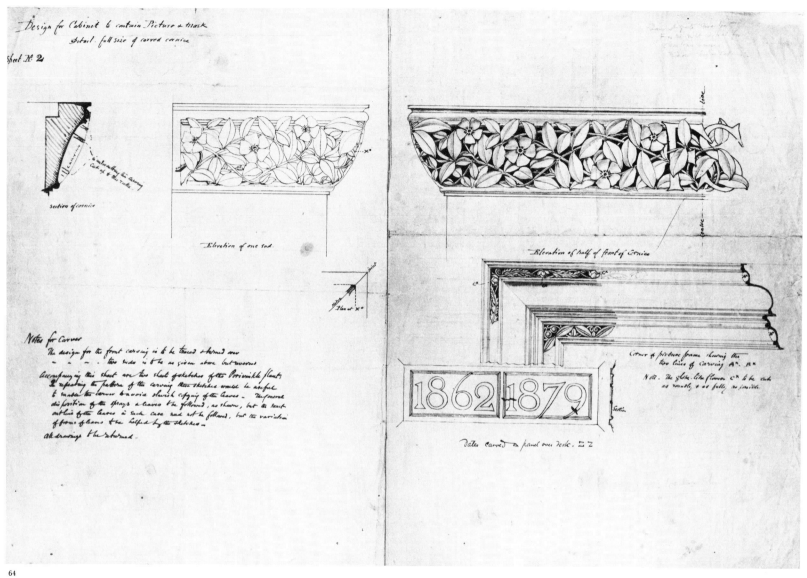

64

(presumably a portrait and death mask). For the carving of the cornice Webb chose the periwinkle as his theme. In the language of flowers, so popular in Victorian times, periwinkles signify the Pleasure of Memory. For the picture frame Webb employed *globe-like flowers* that if, for example, buttercups, would betoken Childhood. The stylized leaves and fruit of the olive refer to Peace. The carving was done by a distinguished carver, James Forsyth, who had done work for Salvin, Sir Gilbert Scott, Nesfield, Shaw and Sir Ernest George. To enable him to avoid slavish copying Webb also sent *two sheets of sketches of the Periwinkle plant* drawn in the garden of the house he had designed for his doctor brother at Welwyn.

Webb made many studies from nature, drawing plants, birds and animals and used them with great naturalism in his designs for tapestries, embroideries and other decorative work. He thought that lack of ornament — 'bareness and baldness' — could be seen to be affected and yet that decoration unless it was really beautiful was worthless.

On the death of his father in 1889, John Yorke inherited Forthampton Court, a large rambling medieval house with eight staircases in which 'every room smelt of something it ought not to — rats, drains &c'[47]. Although it was virtually uninhabitable Webb persuaded his client not to build a new house on a different site as he had first decided but to

repair the old one. It was a job of careful restoration and modest additions that Webb particularly enjoyed.

The drawing room at Forthampton was the upper part of the 15th century hall that at some time before Webb began work had been divided into two storeys. Webb designed a new chimneypiece and panelling and added a bay window. A carpet and wall hangings were got from Morris & Co and a mobile, oak bookcase was made (fig. 65), probably by one of the joiners on the site. Webb used a Maltese cross plan, putting adjustable shelves on three sides and a glazed door on the fourth. The cupboard thus formed may have been used for further books or else for drawing room necessities. For the last seventy years at least, it has contained family memorabilia in the form of scrap-books and photographs and the shelves hold bound volumes of such 19th century serials and journals as *Sundays at Home*, the *Quarterly Review*, the *Journal of the Royal Agriculture Society* and *Bohn's Library* (in 72 volumes). The segmental corners of the bookcase were each braced by two fixed, convex shelves, and the tall, slim form was capped by ogee arches that echo the ogival wind braces of the medieval roof. This crown-like steeple was topped by a crest that in the design seems to depict the family's favourite gun dog. In execution this was changed to the 'lion's head erased proper' of the family coat of arms. The bookcase survives still, though when the hall was re-instated as a single room in 1913 Webb's drawing room decorations were lost.

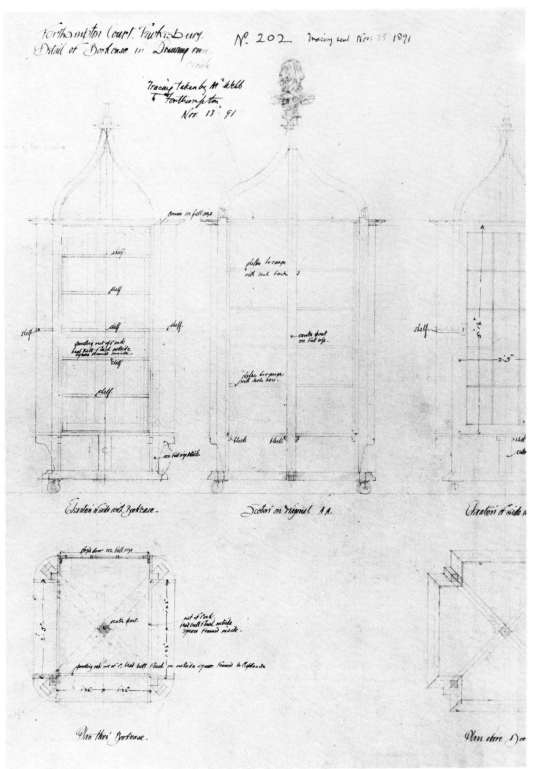

George Gilbert Scott, Junior (1839-1897)

66. Design for a chair for the dining room of the architect's house, 26 Church Row, Hampstead, London *c.* 1874. Pencil on detail paper (1215 x 575) *scale*: full size *h.* 3ft 7ins *w.* 1ft 6ins *d.* 1ft 3¾ins.

67. Sketch of a chair, 1874. Pencil, detail from sketchbook (270 x 370) *scale*: 1½ins to 1ft and full size *h.* 3ft 6½ins *w.* 1ft 5½ins *d.* 1ft 2¾ins.

68. Design for a low sideboard to be made by Watts & Co., 1877. Pencil with brown and blue washes (detail from sheet 660 x 535) *scale*: 2ins to 1ft *h.* 4ft 6ins *w.* 6ft *d.* 1ft 6ins.

69. & 70. Design for a sideboard to be made by Watts & Co., 1877. Pencil and yellow wash (detail from sheet 355 x 255), pencil with black and yellow washes (255 x 355) *scale*: 1in to 1ft *h.* 10ft *w.* 5ft *d.* 2ft.

Scott's earliest and largest house was Garboldisham Manor in Norfolk (1868-73), designed in a mixed Tudor and Jacobean style with mid-17th century elements. His designs for the furniture included a gigantic sideboard, the drawings for which clearly illustrate an initial impulse towards elaborate Jacobean carved ornament that was soon emended. From now on Scott adopted the 'Queen Anne' style for his houses and parsonages and carried it through in his designs for furniture.

'Queen Anne' was not, in fact, a revival of the architecture and applied arts of the period, 1702-14. Rather, it was a mining of 17th and early 18th century details that, freely treated, produced an artistic domestic style which despite occasional foreign borrowings seemed essentially English. In his designs for furniture Scott, as his sketchbooks in the RIBA Drawings Collection show, found his sources in such houses as Haddon Hall and Hardwick Hall and in simple, country-made furniture that he came across in the vestries of out-of-the-way churches. His sketches also reveal his interest in joinery details and his particular fascination with balusters. They suggest too, a search for the quintessential chair of the kind that Morris & Co. found in the rush-bottomed Sussex chair. A low-backed, leather-seated chair that Scott discovered in the "Hospital at Bruges" in 1872 was used, with but a single modification, for the dining room chairs for Garboldisham Manor. Another chair, found at Monks Kirby church (fig. 67) formed the basis for chairs for Scott's own dining room in the early 18th century house in Church Row, Hampstead that he lived in from 1872 (fig. 66). The chairs, and the dining table, survive still.

To secure the kind of articles that he wanted, Scott set up with Bodley and Garner, in 1874, the firm of Watts & Co. His account book[48] shows that he

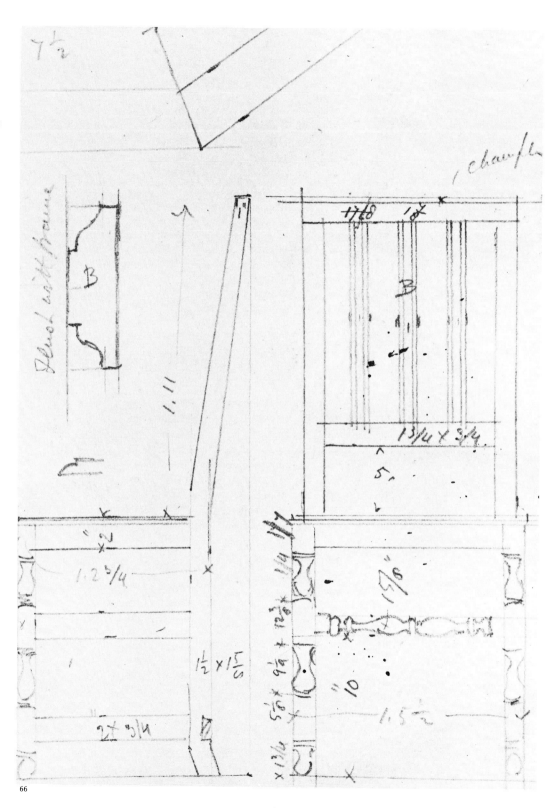

66

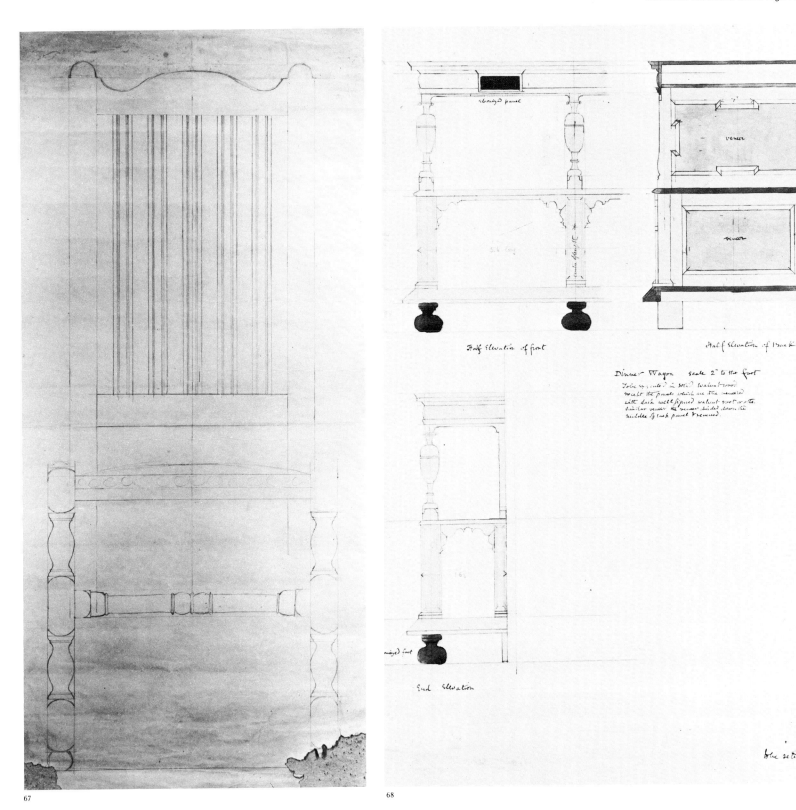

Half Elevation of front

Half Elevation of Back

Dinner Wagon   scale 2" to the foot

End Elevation

67

68

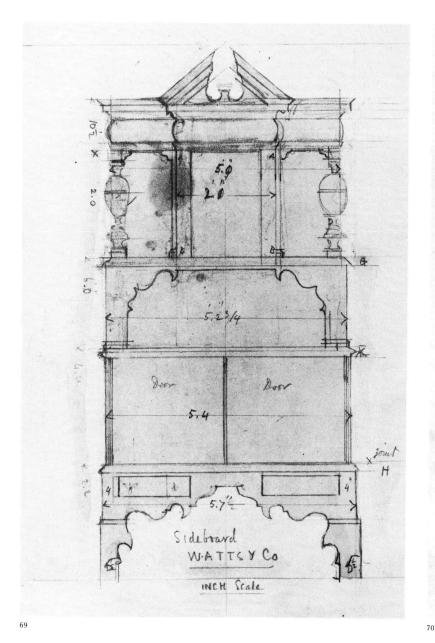

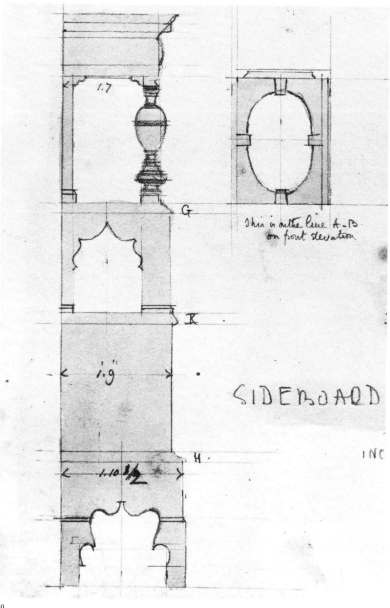

69

70

designed wallpaper, ecclesiastical needlework, tiles and metalwork for these Fine Art Workmen as well as furniture. For two designs for 'dinner waggons' shown here, Scott charged £12. One dinner wagon, or low sideboard, was a free adaptation of a 17th century court cupboard (fig. 68). It was executed in *solid walnut wood* except for the panels which were *veneered with dark well figured walnut root . . . the veneer divided down the middle of each panel & reversed.* The bun feet and geometric panels were ebonized. Another

sideboard, of dresser form, for Watts & Co. (figs. 69 & 70) was made of English walnut and the base cunningly houses two drawers. It shares some of the features of the other, but the open pediment with a pedestal for a pot was borrowed from the 18th century. The source for the oval opening with key-pieces was a door at Windsor Castle that Scott sketched two years before and noted as 'very good'. Scott's borrowings, direct at the start, became increasingly absorbed into his designs. His

understanding of construction was sound and un-doctrinaire. If a wardrobe stood in a recess then the sides could be of painted deal; large tables might have their stretchers reinforced with iron rods and an extensible table at Peterhouse College was opened out by means of a winch. Scott's main concern was with the design of modest, well made, easy-to-live-with furniture.

Plate XIII: see page 97

Plate XIV: see page 97

Plate XV: see page 98

Plate XVI: see page 104

Sir Ernest George (1839-1922)

71. Design for the drawing room at Poles near Thundridge, Hertfordshire for Edmund Smith Hanbury, 1891. Sepia pen and wash (455 x 635) *see* Plate XIII, p.93.

Edmund Smith Hanbury (1850-1913) inherited the Poles estate in 1884. Four years later he resigned his partnership with the brewing firm of Truman Hanbury & Co. and in that same year decided to pull down the 'plain and rather unattractive building of grey, painted brick' that was the old house at Poles and to build anew. Early in 1889 Ernest George, who had been introduced through a mutual friend, was asked to design the new Poles and building work began in March 1890 and was finished by February 1892 at a cost of £38,450.

From 1871 Ernest George had been in partnership with Harold Peto (1854-1933) but it is clear from the diaries kept by Mr and Mrs Hanbury[49] that it was George who had the major responsibility for the design of their house. Regarded by them as a 'first rate artist and designer, much taste, perhaps not very practical' he was very well liked. But Hanbury, found Peto irritating and a 'sham gentleman'. Edmund and Amy Hanbury were discerning clients who had a hand in the choice of style and treatment and in the planning of their house. They visited houses recently designed by George & Peto including the architects' own homes at Streatham Common and in Kensington and they saw and commended George Devey's Hall Place in Kent, built in a Tudor style some years before. Hanbury's diary for 13 June 1889 has the interesting entry 'Talk to George and Peto . . . took them drawings of Spains Hall'. Spains Hall in Essex is a late 16th century house of red brick with stone dressings, mullioned windows and curved gables. Poles (described variously in the architectural press as Jacobean, Elizabethan and based upon 17th century architecture of a more English type than was usual in George's work) was also of red brick with curved gables and dressings and mullioned windows of a warm coloured stone.

The drawing room with its white-painted panelling and enriched plaster ceiling was arranged *enfilade* with the dining room and library so that when the folding doors were opened there was a 120 foot vista. George's perspective of the drawing room shows several pieces of furniture designed by him. Based on late 16th and 17th century sources, the chairs, footstools and cabinet are each of an individual design and are not directly related to each other nor to the room they inhabit save in the general sense of being either of the period or else plausible or (as with the lacquer cabinet) actual accumulations, except, that is, for the cabinet to the

right of the door which with its Ionic pilasters and other enrichments does have some correspondence with the ornament of wall and ceiling. But although, for instance, the height of some of the stretchers coincides with the skirting level, there are none of those unifying details between interior and furniture that are the usual hallmark of architect designed furniture. George's aim was to produce a picturesque effect, an impression of a house lived in by many generations in which the charm of olden days was combined with modern conveniences — Poles was lit by electricity. In terms of furniture this could have been achieved by using antiques and Hanbury's diary does record visits in March 1891 to antique dealers who may have been recommended to him by Ernest George. For the architect and his partner were both avid collectors of furniture, tapestries, carved stone and woodwork, pictures and *objects d'art* of the medieval and Renaissance periods. They were in touch with antique dealers, collected on their travels abroad and were, for example, friends as well as architects to Percy Macquoid the well-known furniture historian. This expertise shows itself in George's designs. The armchair with rudimentary wings was adapted from an early 17th century settee at Knole and a two-seater version was used for Shiplake Court, another of George's country houses. Again, the high-backed armchair was probably based on a chair that belonged to Peto and which appears in a contemporary photograph of his drawing room at 7 Collingham Gardens. None of the pieces are direct copies but rather slightly simplified versions of existing pieces of quality. In these and other of his furniture designs, George avoided the very grandly ornate, drew on sources ranging from the Medieval period to the mid-18th century, and his consistent employment of stretchers showed a concern with structural stability.

Around 1913, the Hanburys left Poles which then became a convent school. The drawing room is now the girls' study room and none of the furniture shown in the perspective survives at Poles.

Ernest Newton (1856-1922)

72. Design for a sideboard for the dining room at Bohun Lodge, East Barnet, Hertfordshire for Mr Gribble, 1884. Pencil and watercolour (535 x 335) *scale*: ½in to 1ft *h.* 11ft 9ins *w.* 10ft 6ins *see* Plate XIV, p.94.

Almost all of Newton's earliest jobs, after he had left Norman Shaw's office in 1879 and set up for himself, were small alterations and additions or the design of a chimneypiece or piece of furniture or the decoration of a room. This sideboard was part of his scheme at Bohun Lodge (built 1775) for a dining room decorated in the 'greenery-yallery' tints of advanced taste of the 1880s. The acanthus frieze is similar to the one painted by William Morris in Newton's additions to Bullers Wood, a few years later. The wallpaper was perhaps Morris's St James's Palace acanthus design and echoes the acanthus frieze of Newton's sideboard. This shrine-like buffet must have been the focal point of the East Barnet dining room that it adorned and the butler's delight. Large (it could scarcely have been taller), it reveals Newton's fondness for the 'half-dome' which he applied to porches, over bow windows, on chimneypieces and in cupboards: here it is seen as a shell-hood. Indeed the sideboard seems to be an anthology of motifs culled from Newton's domestic architecture of the period. Everything, from the scrolled pediment to the frilly apron can be found in the 'Queen Anne' houses that Newton designed with accomplishment before going on to pioneer free Neo-Georgian.

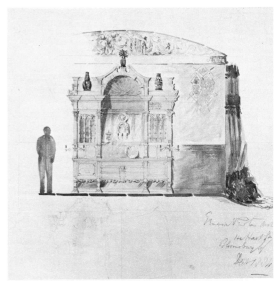

Charles Francis Annesley Voysey (1857-1941)

73. Design for a clock case, for the architect's own use 1895. Pencil, watercolour and gold paint (780 x 555) *scale*: full size *h.* 1ft 7¾ins *w.* 10⅝ins *d.* 7ins *see* Plate XV, p.95.

74. Design for a sideboard for Mrs van Gruisen, 37 Bidston Road, Oxton, Cheshire, 1902. Pen with yellow and blue washes on linen (570 x 395) *scale*: 1in to 1ft and full size *h.* 7ft 2ins *w.* 5ft 6ins *d.* 2ft 1in.

75. Alternative designs for a dining chair, 1902. Pen on linen (770 x 565) *scale*: 1½ins to 1ft and full size *h.* 4ft 6ins and 3ft 4½ins *w.* 2ft *d.* 1ft 7ins.

76. Design for a settle for S.C. Turner, The Homestead, Frinton, Essex, 1907. Pen and yellow wash (400 x 565) *scale*: 1in to 1ft and full size *h.* 2ft 5ins *w.* 5ft 10ins *d.* 2ft 6½ins.

77. Design for a circular folding table for E.J. Horniman MP, Garden Corner, Chelsea Embankment, London, 1907. Pen and yellow wash (735 x 565) *scale*: 1in to 1ft and full size *h.* 2ft 2ins *diam.* 2ft 6ins.

73

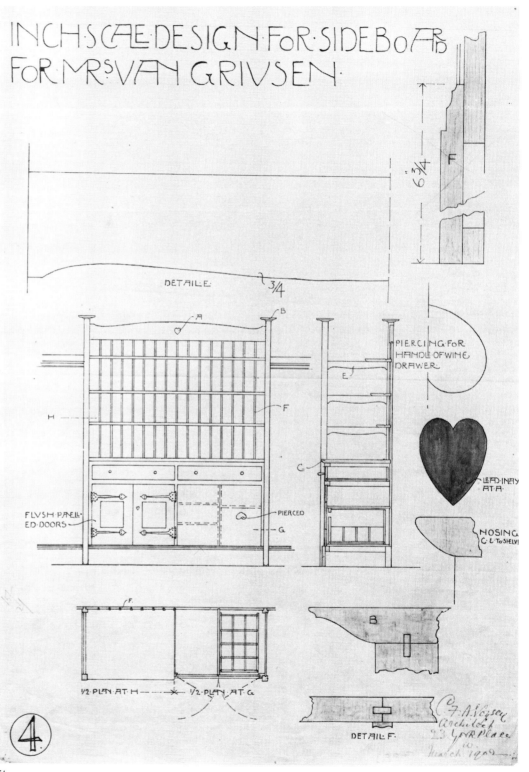

74

Within the compass of house and garden there was very little that Voysey did not design. He took the view that nothing was too unimportant to merit his attention. In a practice that was almost exclusively domestic, Voysey did five 'total design' houses including his own. The distinctive unity and consistency of his designs for houses, furniture, metalwork, wallpapers, textiles, tiles and carpets derived from the 'single-minded way he worked out solutions to functional and visual problems, according to his principle of fitness for purpose, and then re-used the same solutions over a period of years, sometimes modified or elaborated'.[50] Some forms were used, to different scales, for both buildings and furniture. Thus a design for a clock case with slender pilasters, cornice and shallow dome made in January 1895 (fig. 73) is very like a project for a monument to Queen Victoria drawn three weeks later. And both are similar to a design (not as executed) for a stable gateway at Perrycroft of 1893. Another stable gateway, a barometer, cupolas and a clock case in aluminium all share this simple but distinctive architectural form.

The clock case, which was for Voysey himself, was of soft wood and painted by him with a stylized landscape scene. Neither the use of soft wood nor the painted decoration were typical of Voysey. He almost invariably relied on oak 'left clean from the plane' and 'free from all stain or polish' and though he experimented with inlaid, pierced and carved work his most characteristic enrichments were brass strap hinges. Some were elaborate but most, like the openwork heart hinges on Mrs van Gruisen's sideboard (fig. 74), were simple.

The heart, Voysey's best known motif, appears several times on this dresser-sideboard. Another typical feature was the square, capped support carried above the main structure. Borrowed from Mackmurdo, Voysey used it with finely adjusted proportions on bureaux, beds, settles, pianos and staircases as well as for the piers of the Sanderson wallpaper factory. These supports, emphasised by caps, contribute to the definition of parts that characterises Voysey's furniture. Here, the planked back, the corner supports bridged to make a ladder for the shelves, the drawers and the cupboards with their emphatic door furniture provide the elements.

The designs for a *dining chair to be made in oak oiled slightly and fitted with rush seat* show high backed and low backed alternatives for a chair with arms (fig. 75). Both were made in other versions: the lathe-back chair, designed first in 1898, was widely used in Voysey houses. The splat-with-pierced-heart chair was even more popular and Voysey himself owned at least one. First designed in 1902, it was produced in quantity by F.C. Nielsen (who made most of Voysey's furniture between 1901 and 1914) and a

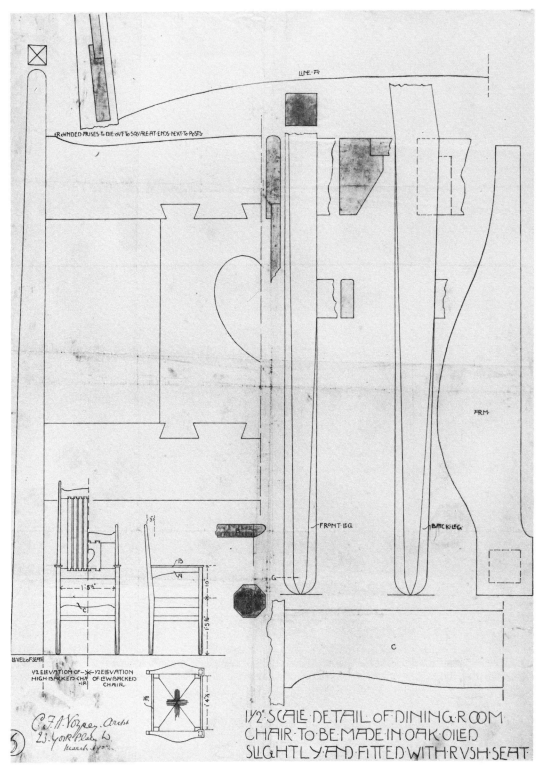

75

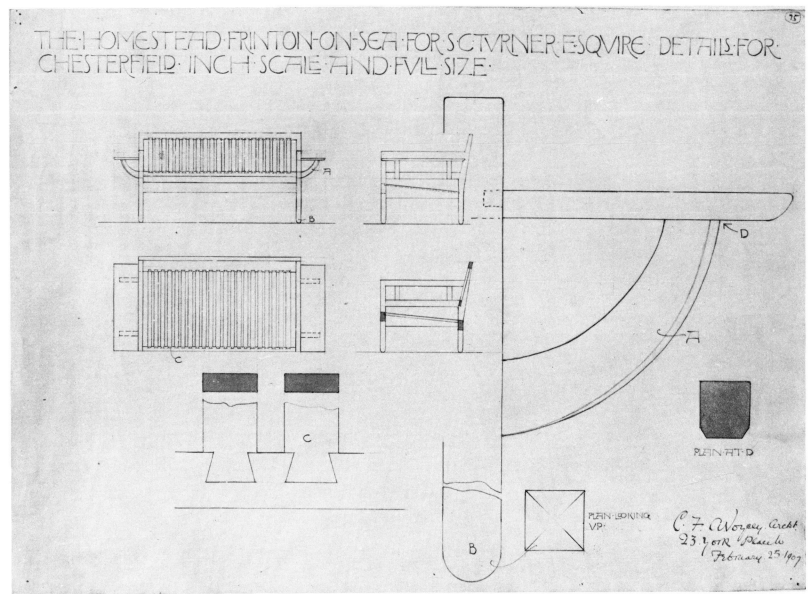

version was produced and sold by Liberty & Co.

The Homestead at Frinton was one of Voysey's 'total designs'. He designed everything from fire tongs to fitted furniture, including a handsome chesterfield or settle (fig. 76). Of oak with a lathe back and seat and quadrant supported elbows, it was placed opposite a billiard table also designed by Voysey. The settle was used (its austerity tempered by cushions) in E.J. Horniman's Chelsea drawing room along with a circular folding table. Again made of oak (fig. 77), this was constructed using only wooden pivots and fixings. Two of the octagonal-sectioned legs were fixed and four were gate legs.

Each was connected to a central boss by six straight stretchers and six curved stretchers that look rather like a trapped spider. The emphasis on legs found here is typical of Voysey, who deliberately stressed the structural elements in his furniture. The quality that he sought, and achieved, was simplicity: 'to know where to stop and what not to do'.

76

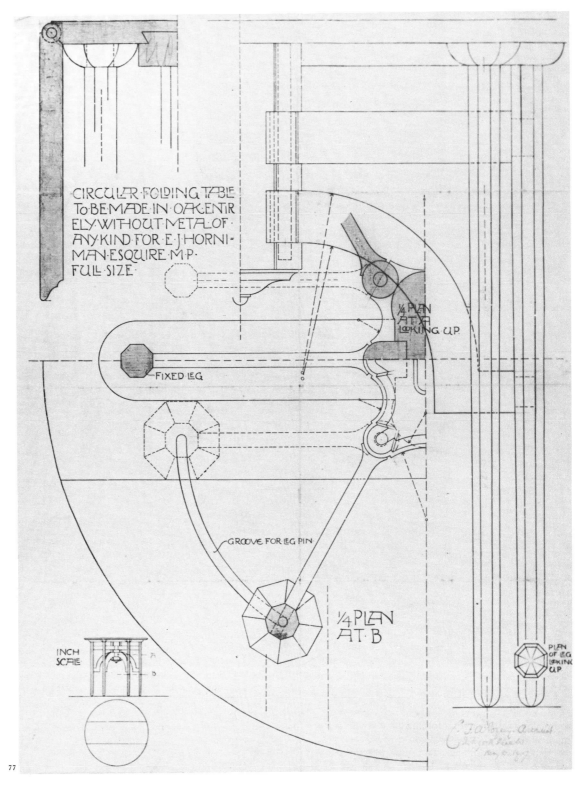

CIRCULAR·FOLDING·TABLE
To·BE·MADE·IN·OAK·ENTIR
ELY·WITHOUT·METAL·OF·
ANY·KIND·FOR·E·J·HORNI-
MAN·ESQUIRE·M·P·
FULL·SIZE·

FIXED·LEG

¼ PLAN
AT·A
LOOKING·UP

GROOVE·FOR·LEG·PIN

¼ PLAN
AT·B

PLAN
OF·LEG
LOOKING
UP

INCH
SCALE

77

78

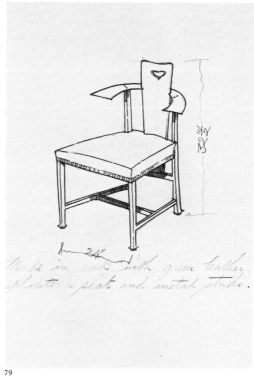

79

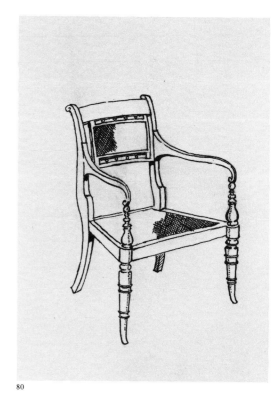

80

George Walton (1867-1933)

Designs for furniture, *c.* 1898-1901. Pen or, pen with brown and green washes in a ruled ledger used as a record book (330 x 230).

78. Holland cabinet *h.* 5ft *w.* 4ft.

79. Abingwood chair *h.* 2ft 8ins *w.* 2ft.

80. Arm chair with cane seat.

81. Beechcroft chair *h.* 4ft 11½ins *d.* 2ft 2ins.

Designs for furniture for Mr Pearce, Alma House, 73 Radon Road, Cheltenham, Gloucestershire, *c.* 1907. Pen and pencil with brown and green washes (255 x 195).

82. Alma sideboard *h.* 4ft 1in *w.* 5ft 6ins *d.* 1ft 9ins.

83. Alma easy chair.

84. Alma coffee stool *h.* 1ft 6ins *d.* 1ft.

The only artistic training Walton ever had was from attending evening classes, probably at the Glasgow School of Art. All the same when he was twenty-one Walton threw up his job in a bank and set up in business as a designer and interior decorator, eventually carrying out architectural commissions. After ten years in Glasgow he moved to London and the Holland cabinet (fig. 78) probably got that name from Walton's Holland Street house in Kensington. He lived there from 1901 though it is likely that the cabinet was designed a year or so earlier. The curved doors with small panes, pronounced cornice and lean lines are characteristic of Walton's early post-Glasgow work. It was executed in unpolished walnut, a wood that suggested to Walton a colour scheme of 'purple & grey with touches of rose colour and silver'.[51]

The Holland cabinet is one of many designs in Walton's record book. Others include the Abingwood chair made in *oak with green leather upholstered seat and metal studs* (fig. 79). This was one of a family of chairs related to the rush-seated chair used by Walton for Miss Cranston's Buchanan Street tearooms (1896-7). Like Voysey, Walton often re-worked earlier designs and the elegant armchair with cane seat and back (fig. 80) also made its first appearance (in an armless version with some

differences in proportion and detail) in Miss Cranston's famous tearooms. Derived from a late 18th century source, it makes a striking contrast with the Arts and Crafts homeliness of the Abingwood. Different again in character was the Beechcroft, (fig. 81) a cheerful, clubbable easy chair that with buttoned brown leather made its debut in the hall of Elm Bank, York (1898).

A commission from Mr Pearce, a dental surgeon, for the complete redecoration of Alma House in Cheltenham in about 1907, stimulated a number of furniture designs. A sideboard[52] with a tall gallery (fig. 82) has a back-piece that continues in another dimension the game of convexity and concavity that Walton plays with drawers and shelf. A screen, dining chairs, sofa and settee as well as the easy chair (fig. 83) and *small oak coffee stool* (fig. 84) shown here were all Alma designs. The leather-upholstered, high-backed easy chair has the elegant simplicity that lies at the heart of Walton's work. The coffee stool with its A monogram and inlaid squares shows the continued influence of the Glasgow school. That style was most strongly expressed in Walton's wall decorations, stained glass, textiles and metalwork but in his furniture is only occasionally found, for instance, in a small area of carved decoration on a cabinet or stool.

81

83

SIDE·BUFFET

To stand against wall opposite fireplace near to serving entrance.

82

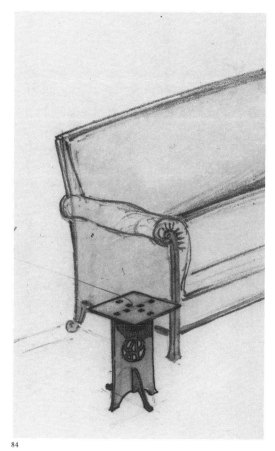

84

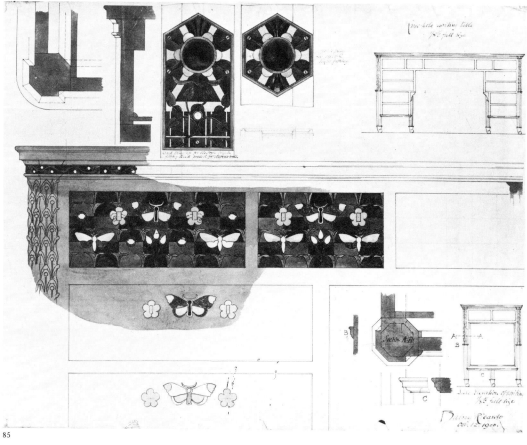

85

Walton's furniture designs, made up in his own workshops, rely, many of them, on existing types. This is especially true of his chairs, where Scottish vernacular, English 17th century, Queen Anne and Regency forms were not reproduced but re-designed with great sensitivity. Walton's 'put-in' furniture — cabinets and sideboards — has less obvious precedents, though the Holland cabinet may have been suggested by the *bonheur du jour*: that small, long-legged, galleried writing table introduced in the mid-18th century. Among contemporaries, Voysey was certainly an influence (and also a close friend), Mackintosh less so. Beyond sources and influences was the innate 'charm, reserve and simplicity' of Walton's designs for furniture, in which 'lucid construction [and] elegance [were combined] to an unusual degree'.[53]

Halsey Ricardo (1854-1928)

85. Design for a writing table for Ernest Debenham, 1900. Sepia pen and coloured washes (510 x 680) *scale*: 1½ins to 1ft and full size *h.* 2ft 6ins *w.* 4ft 10ins *d.* 2ft *see* Plate XVI, p.96.

The knee-hole writing table was designed for Sir Ernest Debenham of the Debenham & Freebody department store. In 1900 he was living in a rented house in Kensington, designed by Halsey Ricardo. Seven years later the Debenhams moved to 8 Addison Road, Kensington, London, a house designed especially for them by Ricardo in a highly personal version of the Arts and Crafts Classical style. The singularity of the colourful glazed exterior was matched by the interior, much of which was clad with William De Morgan tiles as well as mosaic and marble. Reception rooms were panelled in teak or walnut and the library was fitted out in mahogany inlaid with ivory and mother-of-pearl. The flowers and moths theme of the desk was continued and chairs, based on an early Regency style, shared the same rich, mosaic-like decoration.[54]

Ricardo's belief in the 'comfort of colour' and in convenience was maintained in his design for the desk. He abhorred furniture where 'drawers are not made proportionate for their duty',[55] that is, too few and too deep, and here he provides no less than thirteen shallow drawers. Apart from the bayleaf enrichment of the uprights, the desk's chief adornments were the marquetry panels. These were designed in a chequerboard pattern overlaid with iridescent moths and green, lily-like plants. Marquetry plates for an electric wall plug (a bell push was designed in the same materials) provide the final touch.

Plate XVII: see page 107

Plate XVIII: see page 107

86

87

Edgar Wood (1860-1935)

86. Design for the dining room, Birkby Lodge, Birkby Hall Road, Huddersfield, for Mr Norton, 1901. Pencil and watercolour (280 x 445) *see* Plate XVII, p.105.

87. Designs for two mirrors, *c.* 1928. Pencil with coloured washes and gold paint (480 x 620) *scale:?* full size *h.* 1ft. 6½ins *w.* 10¾ins and *h.* 1ft. 6½ins. *w.* 11¼ins. *see* Plate XVIII, p.106.

The dining room at Birkby Lodge, (fig. 86) part of Wood's extensions to an existing house, was in his most cogent Arts and Crafts manner. It expressed that Movement's belief that every detail should be integrated into the overall design and Wood's view that in domestic interiors 'the line should be drawn sharply and logically between structure and portability and that the dominant note shall always be that of structure, reducing as far as possible the degree and extent of the movable'.[56] So easel pictures were out, for not only were they portable but they also introduced an artistic intention unrelated to the architecture. But mural paintings avoid 'any sense of detachment, unfixedness, or looseness' and an important element of Wood's scheme was the frieze showing the Arthurian legend of the Holy Grail. Probably designed by F.W. Jackson, it is likely that Wood had a hand in its execution.[57]

The semicircular windows were placed high for 'windows which are intended for exterior prospects are . . . destroyers of ideal decorative effects'. For that reason, no doubt, the garden door has decorative glass and curtains. Wood's intention was to create an enclosed world in which the 'architectural sense shall . . . be dominant'. Here, everything subscribed to accentuate the walls: the light coloured ceilings, the arrangement of the carpet and so on. Furniture and objects not designed by the architect were carefully selected and integrated by the over-riding use of green.

The sturdy three-stage sideboard (visually united to the panelling by height and the use of a similar chequer pattern) was toned to a silvery grey and a decoration of inlaid, stained and coloured woods was given to the upper doors. It would not have seemed out of place in King Arthur's banqueting hall. The ceiling beams were painted white and decorated with abstract patterns painted in yellow.

Wood was acutely sensitive to the 'emotional and sensual faculties' of colour decoration and he saw nothing sacrilegeous in applying it even to hardwoods: 'materials themselves are not the dominant note . . . the greatest accent . . . should be . . . human expression'. At least as early as 1914, Wood had devised strikingly abstract decoration that seems to anticipate Art Deco. He used it to integrate building, contents and garden and most successfully

in two houses that he built for himself in Cheshire (1914-16) and later in Italy (1932), where he had gone after his retirement in 1922. An *artiste manqué*, Wood was nevertheless among the most advanced architects of the early 20th century. His flat concrete roofed, unhistoricist house at Stafford (1908) made him one of Pevsner's 'pioneers'. A legacy gradually allowed Wood to relinquish his practice and when he retired to Italy he devoted himself to painting and to designing painted decoration for furniture. Much of this he executed himself but some designs were sent to London to be carried out by Sheldon Williams. The designs were for the decoration of tables, chests of drawers and mirrors, in patterns that may have had their source in Arab ornament.

In Wood's designs for two mirrors (fig. 87), form and decoration are fused in an intricate geometry, the angular, stepped shapes of the frames complemented by the colourful abstract decoration. Wood's method, as conveyed to Sheldon Williams,[58] was to apply two coats of white paint, rub down, apply a thin coat of Prussian blue with a stipple brush and when dry put on a layer of varnish. Then the design was painted on, the gold lines first, with a small sable brush "cut to a few hairs as needful". The enamel colours followed.

Richard Barry Parker (1867-1947)

88. Design for the living room, Hill Top, Caterham, Surrey for W.E. Steers, *c.* 1905. Watercolour (250 x 390) *see* Plate XIX, p.115.

89. Design for an armchair, *c.* 1906. Print with brown and green washes added (360 x 235) *scale*: 1in to 1ft *h.* 4ft 1½ins *w.* 2ft *d.* 2ft.

When Wilfred Steers, after nearly thirty years in South Africa, returned home and commissioned Parker and Unwin (Parker seems to have had the major role especially in the interiors) to design a house for him on the windiest and most exposed site that could be found in Surrey, he must have seemed an ideal client, for he allowed Parker to design every detail of the furnishings. Steers was an 'apostle of health'[59] and his gymnasium, exercise lawn and swimming pool all helped to keep him 'in the most perfect condition'. He chose his architects after reading their book on *The Art of Designing a Home* (1901). In it, they claimed for their work a 'complete unity and absolute harmony between all the parts, such as can only be obtained when a house, its decorations and furniture are all designed by one man — or at least under the supervision of one man'. The living room should be the centre of family life, accommodating all activities and if it 'is to be comfortable it *must* have recesses. There is a great charm in 'a room broken up in plan . . . [where] there is always something *round the corner*'. And in such a room 'completeness, comfort and repose' are achieved 'largely by means of fixtures'.

The large, irregularly shaped living room at Hill Top (fig. 88) with two ingles and a bow window had 'with the exception of two or three occasional tables and chairs . . . no loose furniture but the walls are fitted with convenient writing-tables, drawers, cupboards, shelves and recesses' and a pianola-piano. Parker's perspective shows the dining and sitting areas, their geometry stressed throughout. In the arched window recess, the settle follows the contours of the bow window in which stands a circular gate-leg table on a circular rug. In contrast, the ingle is defined by strong horizontals and verticals, an angularity repeated in details such as the tiles and in the book cupboard-cum-table with copper oil lamp. This characteristically multi-purpose piece of furniture was designed with an almost brutal simplicity. Parker did not want 'all trace of [tool] & human hand lost in mere smoothness and mechanised finish' and prefered the 'simplest, most direct . . . construction'. At Hill Top, as at other Parker and Unwin houses, many of the fittings were made by J.P. White of Bedford.

Much of Parker and Unwin's furniture, in particular their rush-bottomed chairs, sturdy dining tables and dressers, was derived from what might

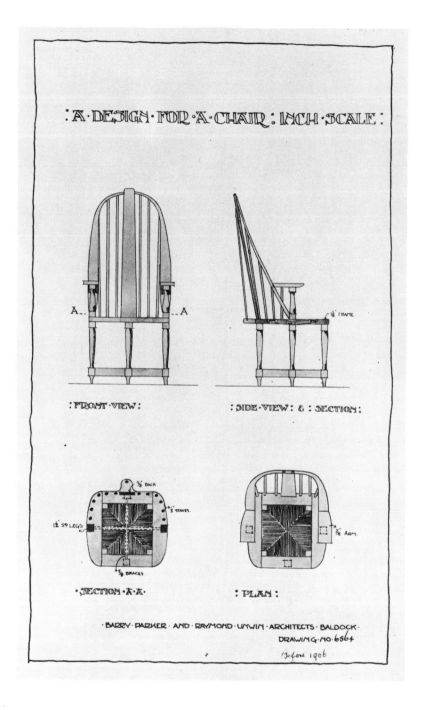

89

have been found in a farmhouse kitchen. However, the design for a chair shown here (fig. 89) is not quite the simple country article that a first impression suggests. It is a very mannered version of the traditional hoop-backed Windsor chair. But the saddle-shaped solid wood seat has been replaced by a drop-in rush seat, the bentwood hoop is flattened and joined to a Voysey-type splayed arm and, most surprising of all, the legs are arranged north-south-east-west.

Sir Edwin Lutyens (1869-1944)

90. Design for a bed, dressing table and armchair for Edward Hudson, Deanery Garden, Sonning, Berkshire, 1902. Pencil with brown and green crayon (570 x 790) *scale*: 1in to 1ft Bed *h.* 7ft *w.* 5ft 7½ins *l.* 6ft 6ins, dressing table *h.* 2ft 8ins *w.* 4ft 1½ins *d.* 1ft 8½ins, armchair *h.* 3ft 3ins *w.* 2ft 2ins *d.* 1ft 7½ins.

91. Design for a table for the kitchen at Castle Drogo, Drewsteignton, Devonshire, for Julius C. Drewe 1924. Pen on tracing paper (detail from sheet 650 x 685) *scale*: 1½ins to 1ft *h.* 2ft 8½ins *diam.* 6ft 5ins.

92-99 Designs for chairs for Viceroy's House, New Delhi, India, 1925-30. Pen (details from sheets, the largest 735 x 1050) *scale*: 3ins to 1ft. 92. *h.* 3ft 4½ins *w.* 1ft 8ins *d.* 1ft 6ins, 93. *h.* 3ft 0¾ins *w.* 2ft 2ins *d.* 1ft 9⅜ins, 94. *h.* 2ft 11½ins *w.* 2ft *d.* 1ft 10½ins, 95. *h.* 2ft 9⅝ins *w.* 1ft 6⅝ins *d.* 1ft 9⅞ins, 96. *h.* 3ft 2ins *w.* 2ft 3 ins *d.* 1ft 8¾ins, 97. *h.* 2ft 9½ins *w.* 2ft 6ins *d.* 1ft 8½ins, 98. *h.* 3ft 4¾ins *w.* 2ft 11⅝ins *d.* 1ft 11¾ins, 99. *h.* 3ft 2½ins *w.* 3ft 3ins *d.* 2ft.

Lutyens designed a wide range of domestic furniture, including garden seats, kitchen furniture, dolls' house furniture, pianos, light fittings, clocks and the occasional oddity such as a billiard table made from chalk. In only a very few instances did he design all the furniture for a building: Viceroy's House, New Delhi had almost all the furniture required in the state and vice-regal apartments designed in the Lutyens office and Marsh Court, Hampshire, Campion Hall, Oxford and the Queen's Dolls' House are other examples of more or less total design. The inspiration for Lutyens's furniture designs developed from vernacular sources to 17th and 18th century sources. The initial influence, though perhaps a slight one, must have come from George & Peto to whom Lutyens was briefly apprenticed. More profound was the influence of Gertrude Jekyll who furnished Munstead Wood (the house Lutyens designed for her) from her collection of country furniture.

It was through Miss Jekyll that Lutyens received the commission to design Deanery Garden for Edward Hudson. Although Hudson, the proprietor of *Country Life*, collected antique furniture Lutyens designed some pieces for him. A bed with *oak canopy* and *bright iron posts* had a headboard whose form was perhaps suggested by the double-headed top and finials of a William and Mary cabinet or a double-back settee of the same period. The bosom-like shape (used at about the same time for a chimneypiece at Marsh Court) was repeated in the scallop-edged canopy and frieze. The side elevation of the bed has a feintly pencilled-in recumbent

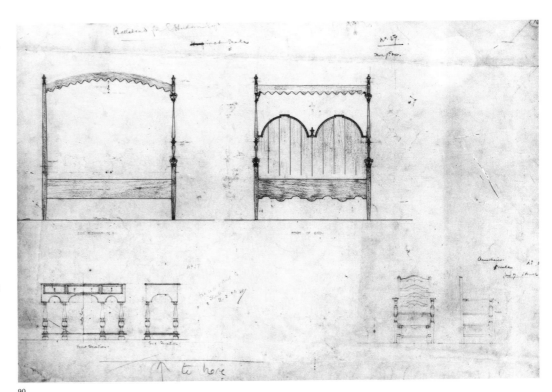

90

figure apparently contemplating an enormous bed bug. The dressing table with baluster legs and curved stretchers owes a debt to late 17th century sources. The rush seated ladderback chair with its shapely turned legs was a lively interpretation of a vernacular type. Bed, table and chair (fig. 90) were all made by Walter Skull & Son of High Wycombe.

Castle Drogo, despite reductions to the original scheme, was twenty years abuilding (1910 to 1930). When he eventually moved in, the owner brought his own furniture with him and the only pieces that Lutyens was required to design were those for the kitchen. Huge, sturdy dressers, plate and vegetable racks, a mortar and pestle, chopping block and work tables were made of unstained oak by local carpenters. Under a raised circular skylight stood (and still stands) a circular table with six turned legs and a circular stretcher (fig. 91). Lutyens may have used a late 17th century precedent for the form of the table or he may have arrived at it independently. Details such as the dowels left proud were a Lutyens mannerism that went back at least as far as the joinery work for Shere Lodge (1894) and was used for the drawing table that he designed for himself (*c.* 1898) and that was made of softwood, stained green.

Two committees were set up (one in London and the other in India) to advise on the furnishings for the hundreds of rooms of Viceroy's House, New Delhi (1912-30). Part of their job was to choose examples of antique furniture for reproduction by Indian craftsmen. Lutyen's office also designed a huge number of pieces[60] basing many of them, to a greater or lesser extent, on historic sources. Thus an instruction on a drawing for a stool for the anteroom to the ballroom reads 'See also Dictionary of English Furniture Vol III, page 173, fig. 53' and when checked against the book by P. Macquoid and R. Edwards (published by Country Life in 1924) reveals that a Chippendale-type window stool with scrolled ends has been exactly copied down to the leather upholstery garnished with nails. The state chairs for the Durbar Hall had William and Mary details while the chairs for His Excellency's sitting room (fig. 92) were directly based on a familiar Queen Anne type. For writing chairs, Lutyens again used well known types including a corner chair of about 1730 and a writing chair with scroll arms of around 1715 (fig. 93). His cane-seated armchair for a guest bedroom (fig. 94) relied on late 18th century precedents while the occasional chairs for the ballroom (fig. 95) suggest a source of about 1805.

Her Excellency's breakfast room was a sixteen-sided room with eight three-quarter circle side tables and, in the centre, an eight-sided table with eight chairs. These chairs (fig. 96) with their truncated triangular seats (no doubt very uncomfortable to sit on) and compass-drawn fretwork backs and front supports responded strongly to the geometry of a singular room.

For the state supper room, Lutyens designed an armchair with a reticulated, compass-organised back, curved arms and seat and straight tapered legs (fig. 97). An easy chair for the south drawing room has the scalloped back and sides, loose cushions and bell-shaped feet of an Indian throne (fig. 98). But the height and width dictated a European sitting position rather an Indian one. On the nearby loggia, those in search of cool breezes and a chota peg might relax on generously proportioned cane chairs with folding arms. (fig. 99).

Viceroy's House was designed in a synthesis of Eastern and Western architecture and some of the furniture, for what was Lutyens's largest and most comprehensive scheme, reflects this amalgam of British Imperial sources. A table in the annexe to the state ballroom was carved with elephant heads and another has tusk-like supports. A design for Her Excellency's bed has carved Indian dancers whose skirts are the traditional bell-shaped feet found on Indian furniture. The aim seems to have been to design some pieces of furniture, usually in the public and state rooms, that subtly offered hints of Indian splendour. While in the viceregal and other apartments, the impression was to be of a gradual accumulation of furniture and objects such as any great country house in England might reveal.

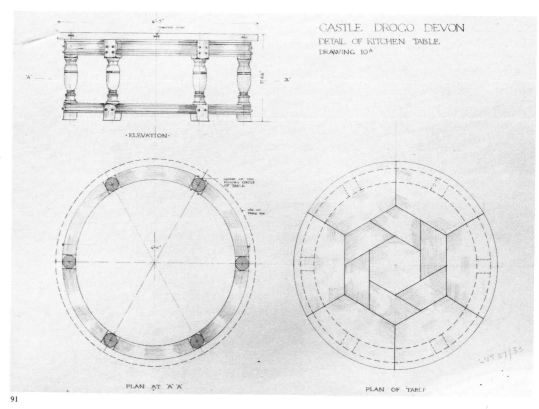

91

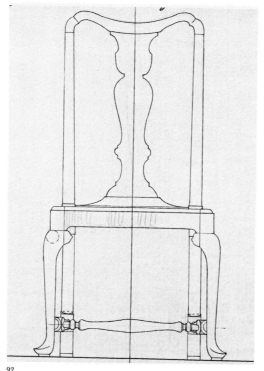

92

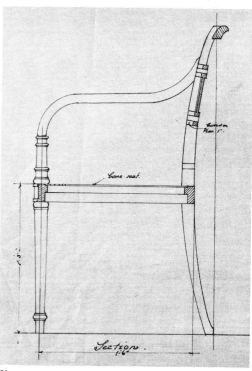

94

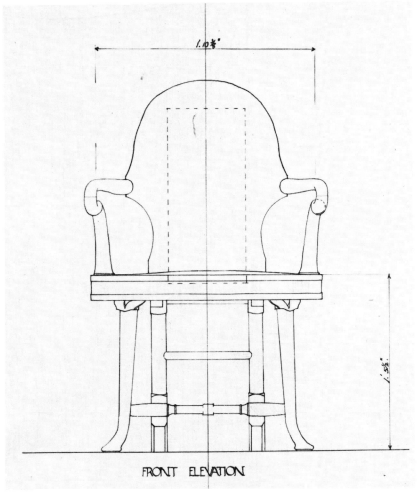

FRONT ELEVATION

93

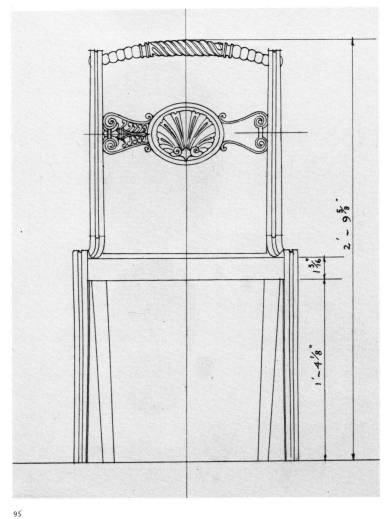

95

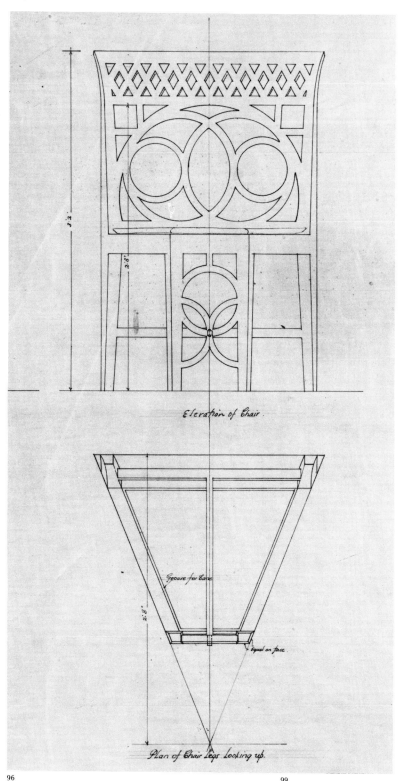

Elevation of Chair.

Groove for Cane

Equal on face.

Plan of Chair Legs Looking up.

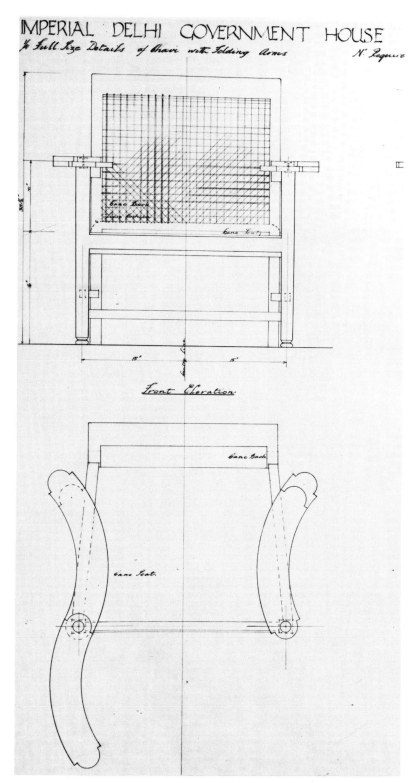

IMPERIAL DELHI GOVERNMENT HOUSE

½ Full Size Details of Chair with Folding Arms   N. Square

Cane Back

Cane Seat

Front Elevation

Cane Back

Cane Seat

96

99

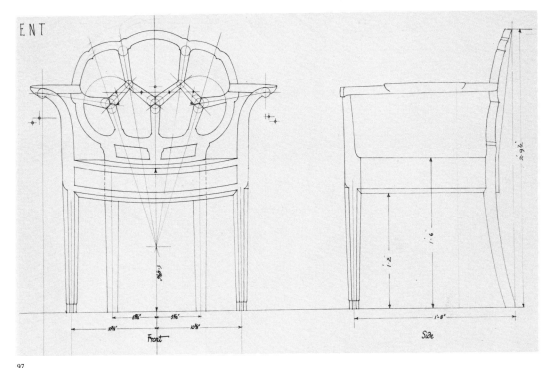

97

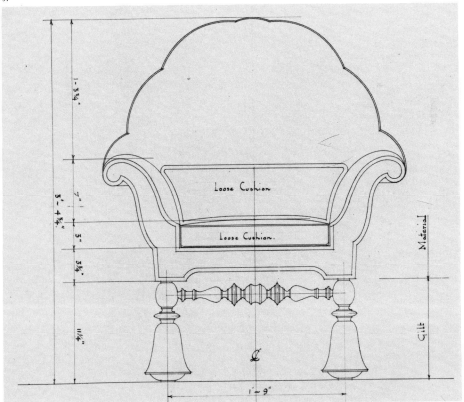

98

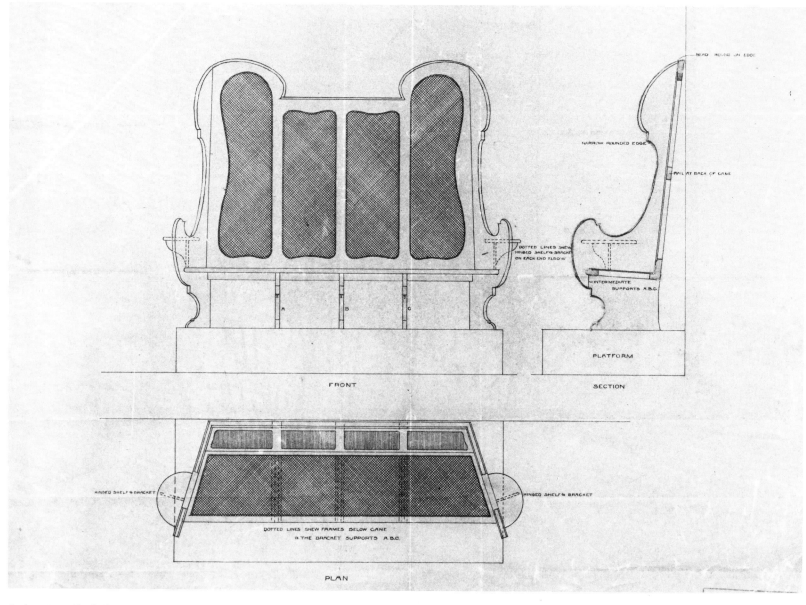

FRONT   SECTION

PLAN

Arthur Beresford Pite (1861-1934)

100. Design for a billiard room settle for J.D. Tremlett, *c.* 1905. Pen with pink and brown washes and some pencil on tracing paper (510 x 525) *scale*: 1in to 1ft *h.* 6ft 3ins *w.* 8ft 8ins *d.* 2ft 9ins.

Architecturally, Beresford Pite played a lone hand. He introduced (with Belcher) Grand Manner Baroque but by the time everyone else was doing it 'he was practising Grecian purity in Euston Square [and] when Grecian purity had been adapted for the million,[61] he was re-reviving Baroque. Pite's design

for a settle shows a similar perversity. The only real difference between a billiard room settle or sofa and that for any other room is that it is placed on a platform. But since in most households the billiard room was regarded as an exclusively male refuge, it was usually furnished in an appropriately robust fashion. However, Pite's *light oak and cane* settle with its Rococo curves has a feminine air (shared by his orchidaceous wallpaper designs) that would not have made it out of place in a boudoir. Still, the hinged shelves on the elbows would have been handy for the gentlemen's whisky-and-soda. And, if

it was intended for a hot climate (Pite did work in West Africa and the Near East) the use of cane was entirely appropriate.

Plate XIX: see page 108

Plate XX: see page 124

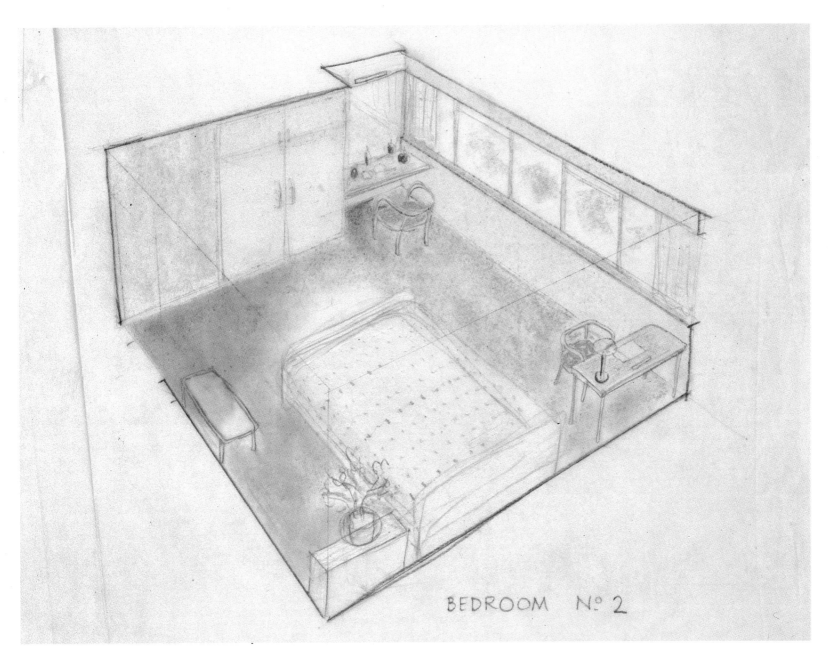

BEDROOM No 2

Plate XXI: see page 137

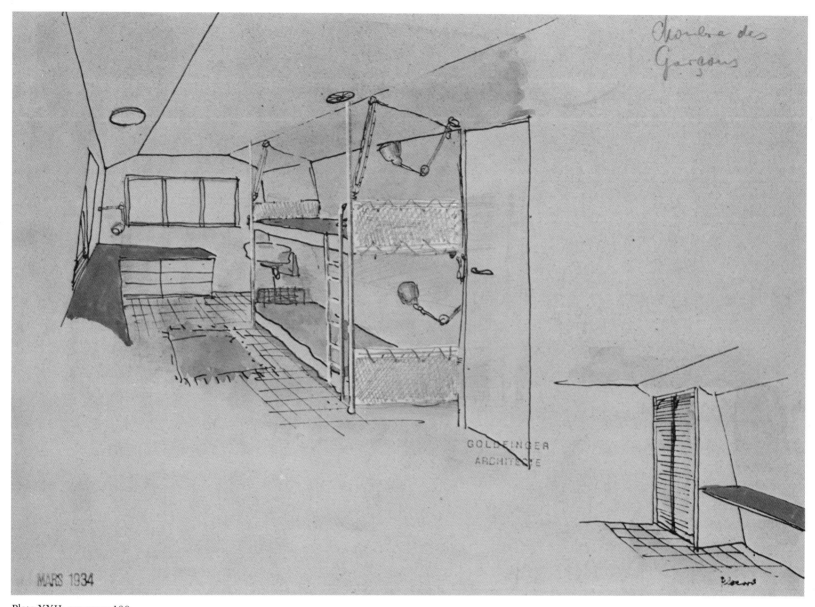

Plate XXII: see page 130

Edwin Alfred Rickards (1872-1920)

101. Design for a sideboard, *c.* 1912. Pencil and watercolour (545 x 835) *scale*: 3ins to 1ft *h.* 4ft 4ins *w.* 9ft 3ins.

Few designs in this book reveal so clearly the author's character as does Rickards's design for a sideboard. A 'draughtsman and designer of exuberant fancy',[62] E.A. Rickards was the master of a full-blown Baroque more Continental than English in its fluency and assertiveness. The sideboard, 'a typical example of his many essays in furniture'[63], was executed in quartered walnut with gilt bronze mounts and may have been designed for Arnold Bennett. The two men were close friends and when,

in 1912, the writer left France and returned to England, buying a house at Thorpe-le-Soken in Essex, it seems almost certain that Rickards helped in its restoration and lavish decoration.

Rickards's sideboard in the French rococo style is a complex affair. The galleried top, aligned to an existing dado rail, is supported by three elements: a serpentine-fronted, four drawer commode with cabriole corners and two *bombé* commodes (or pedestal cabinets). This three-part organisation comes from the sideboard-table-flanked-by-pedestals-grouping introduced by Robert Adam and, combined with the use of French commodes (in the 18th century, essentially drawing room furniture) might be seen as an example of Rickards's

remarkable wit. Accompanying chairs were designed with equal verve and share the sideboard's scallop shell decoration.

103

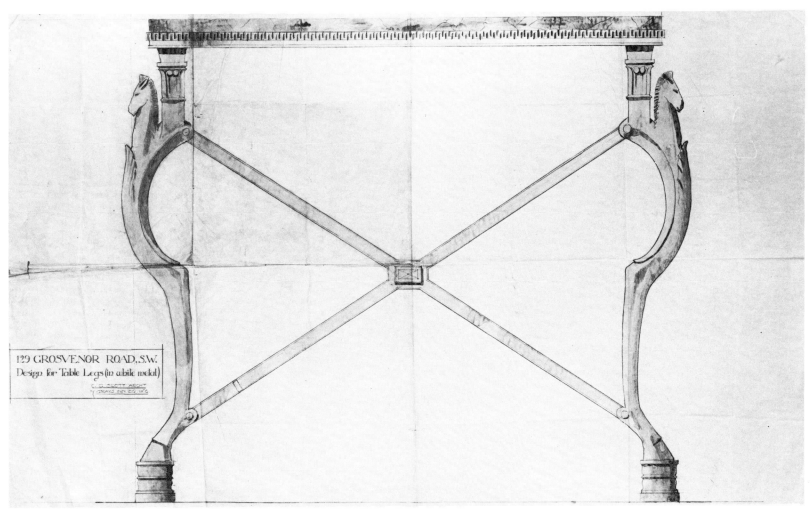

102

Sir Giles Gilbert Scott (1880-1960)

Designs for furniture for the Hon. Arthur Stanley, MP, 129 Grosvenor Road, London c. 1915.

102. Table. Pencil with grey and blue washes (1055 x 1520) *scale*: full size *h*. 2ft 8⅜ins *w*. 3ft 3½ins.

103. Cabinet. Pencil and coloured washes (380 x 460) *scale*: 1½ins to 1ft *h*. 4ft 1in *w*. 5ft 3ins *d*. 11ins.

In 1912 Giles and Adrian Gilbert Scott were asked by Arthur Stanley, a Tory MP and philanthropist, to design him a house on the site of a disused builder's yard on the north bank of the Thames at Pimlico. The brief was as unusual as the site. Stanley, crippled by rheumatic fever, was confined to an invalid chair and the house was to be planned and detailed with this in mind. Further, the client seems to have persuaded his architects to look to Antique

precedents for their design. Though reared in the Gothic tradition, they responded with enthusiasm producing a house that behind a 'moderne' Georgian front concealed a stoa and peristyle. Giles went to Pompeii and there sketched bronze tripods, vases, hanging lamps, reliefs, chairs and benches, and details of wall treatment. The results can be seen in the furniture and decoration of Stanley's house, all of which was designed by Giles Scott. For the legs of a marble-topped table (fig. 102.) Scott closely adapted the details of a bronze folding tripod that he had sketched at Pompeii. The table was probably intended for the 20 x 60 foot River Room that overlooked the Thames. That room had grey and white painted walls and ceilings, black carpeted floor with white marble surround: the door and light fittings were in a simulated 'old greened bronze'[64] while windows and furniture were finished in a dull silver. The same finish was proposed for a cabinet

(possibly unexecuted) that had necessarily to depart from Antique sources (fig. 103.). The doors to the cabinet share the same arrangement of glazing bars as the windows to the room and these taut borders emphasise a rectilinearity that is relieved in the cabinet by cavetto mouldings and cabriole legs. Oblong drawer pulls on the three slim drawers of the stand and circular door knobs continue the same game. The house was an exercise in geometry, the right angles discreetly offset by the oval form of an ante-room or by fluted columns or tub chairs. A secondary organising principle was the system of framing and sub-framing: thus contrasting colours and materials, pilasters, sunken panels, architraves, reeded mouldings to incised lines and bordered, edged and margined floors, ceilings, walls and openings in an awesome consistency that was both paralleled and relieved by the furniture.

Sir Edward Maufe (1883-1974)

104. Design for a table for the architect's own use, Shepherd's Hill, Buxted, Sussex, *c.* 1927-9. Pencil with brown, green and red crayon and pen inscriptions on tracing paper (525 x 590) *scale:* 1in to 1ft and full size *h.* 2ft 5in *w.* 2ft 6ins *l.* 6ft 6ins.

In 1926 Prudence and Edward Maufe bought a dilapidated Georgian farm and spent the next three years in remodelling, decorating, furnishing and landscaping a home that was then to remain little changed for nearly fifty years. Shepherd's Hill was the expression of Maufe's very personal style. Described once as 'modernity with manners' and seen at its best in his work between the wars, it was influenced by Lethaby, Lutyens and by contemporary Swedish architecture and design. Some of the hallmarks of Maufe's style included a concern with balance, a reliance on the inherent colour and texture of materials and an economy and discretion of detail. His design for a table has the simplicity that 'requires much thought and art'.[65] Though based on country furniture of the 17th century its proportions and the finesse of its details give it an elegance that is not at all rustic.[66] Made of English walnut, Ibus board (a manufacturer's trade name for blockboard) and Swedish green marble, it was used as a writing table and placed in front of a tall sash window in The Room — as the Maufes called their principal living room. The Room embodied their views on decoration: scrubbed oak floor boards, roughish textured plaster walls distempered grey-cream, low toned colourings, diffused light, a seemly fireplace, good sculpture combined with a minimum amount of furniture well spaced out. Other furniture designed by Maufe for his house might be described as an amalgam of Arts and Crafts and Art Deco with the occasional use of a flat Baroque motif borrowed from one of Maufe's Swedish mentors, Ragnar Ostberg.

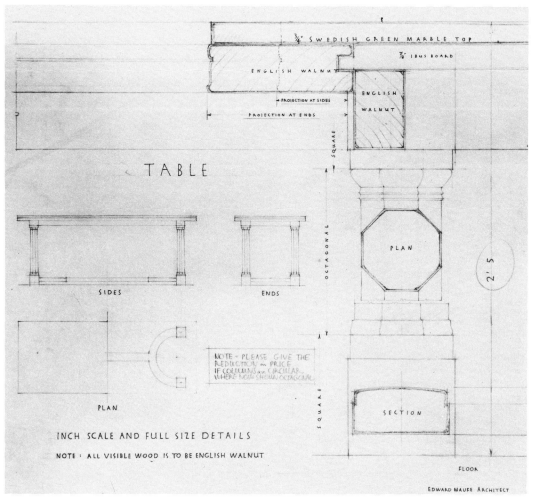

104

Oliver Hill (1887-1968)

105. & 106. Designs for two settees for the music room 40 Devonshire Mansions, Piccadilly, London, for Mr and Mrs Albert Levy, 1927. Pencil with brown and green washes and silver paint; pencil with brown and yellow washes and silver paint (both, 275 x 380) *w.* 8ft and 5ft 6ins respectively.

107. Design for a cocktail cabinet for Miss Evelyn Laye, 36 Grove Court, St John's Wood, London, 1929. Pencil and coloured washes (295 x 190) *scale*: 1in to 1ft *h.* 6ft 10ins *w.* 3ft *see* Plate XX, p.116.

Designs for furniture for Mr and Mrs Eustace Thornton, Hampton Lodge, Seale, Survey, 1931.

108. Chair. Pencil and coloured washes (200 x 145).

109. Circular table. pencil and brown washes (195 x 160).

110. & 111. Designs for bedroom furniture. Pencil and crayon (details from 2 pages of an album, 270 x 385).

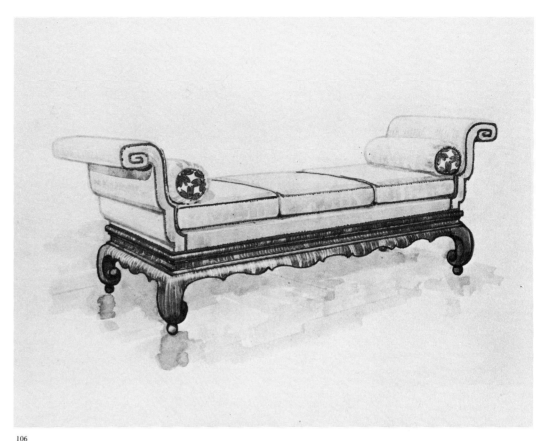

105

106

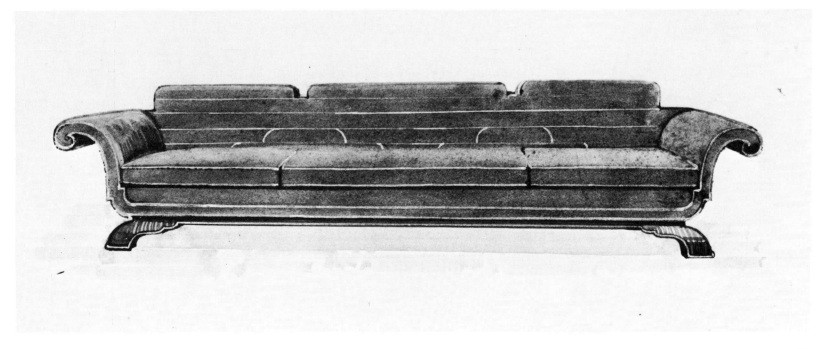

107

108

109

Oliver Hill, once described as 'the most facile and versatile of . . . architects' was the unembarrassed practitioner of many styles. And whilst his furniture, *décor* and upholstery was as eclectic as his buildings, recurrent themes can be detected in Hill's interior designs. These include a tendency to combine expensive, fashionable finishes (exotic veneers, silver leaf, lacquers) with apparently simple forms borrowed from 17th and 18th sources as well as from contemporaries, and a theatricality that attracted clients but alienated more serious architects and designers.

Hill's earliest decorative scheme (for a library, *c.* 1913) was in a Wrenish Baroque. A decade later he was producing furniture in walnut, silvered wood, red lacquer and figured velvet that can best be described as Curzon Street Baroque. 'Low and broad and baroque' was how Professor Reilly[67] described the rather Chinese-looking settees (figs. 105 & 106) designed for Mr and Mrs Albert Levy's music room. This was panelled in laminated wood (a new material) veneered with French walnut bleached grey, edged with silver and painted by George Sheringham with landscape scenes 'after the manner of a coromandel screen'. The same wood was used for the settees which were upholstered in grey-green velvet and made by Howard & Sons Ltd of Berners Street, London. Hill's decorations for the

rest of the twenty-five-room flat in the newly built Devonshire House were done on an apparently limitless budget. Encouraged by the sumptuous ensembles displayed at the recent Decorative Arts Exhibition in Paris, Hill employed a wealth of materials (marbles of several kinds, alabaster, onyx, verdite, malachite, lapis lazuli and engraved black glass) to help create a home for his 'austere trillionaire' client.

Hill's lighthearted design for a cocktail cabinet (fig. 107) was done as part of the alterations and decorations to Evelyn Laye's flat in St John's Wood. Miss Laye was then starring in Ivor Novello's 'Lilac Time' and 'Bitter Sweet' and the cocktail cabinet does express something of the brittle artificiality of the musical stage. Over an ivory lacquered table with scalloped top, Hill placed a hanging cupboard with the same profile, lacquered in cream 'picked out in ivory'. Inside the cupboard (lacquered black, picked out in red) scallopy shelves imprison the glasses, bottles, decanters and cocktail shaker that are reflected in the blue-black glass lining acid-etched, at the bottom, with twin cupids' heads. Except for the grand piano, Hill seems to have designed (and Howard & Sons to have made) almost all of the furniture for the flat. The walls were silver leafed (with a 'faint suggestion of peach' for the bedroom) or painted cream and ivory. Some furniture had a

scumbled silver finish but most was lacquered in red, yellow, green or black and the tables had glass tops. Hill added Lalique light fittings, skin rugs, mirrored console tables and a lot of taffeta and tassels and (the final touch) Miss Laye's dolls were dressed to match the curtains and cushions.[68]

Though a millionaire, Eustace Thornton was a man of 'simple habits'. He sought Hill's advice after the purchase of a neglected house in Surrey and so impressed was Thornton and his wife Mary by 'Mr Hill's competence and taste . . . that they appointed him as their adviser in everything made or purchased for their home, even down to a hand mirror or a hairbrush'.[69] They were persuaded to throw out their existing furniture and their collection of mid-Victorian paintings and to start again with Hill-designed furniture and some of Ivon Hitchen's flower studies.

For the hall at Hampton Lodge, Hill re-used his version of an 18th century wheel back chair (fig. 108) that he had designed two years before for Essendon Place, a Georgian mansion. The same Neo-Georgian tendency was evident in the urn-shaped support to a circular table of weathered sycamore and padouk made by Howard & Sons (fig. 109). Other urns appeared on standard lamps and pilaster-like fluting on chair and table legs whilst the garden seats had Chinese Chippendale fretted

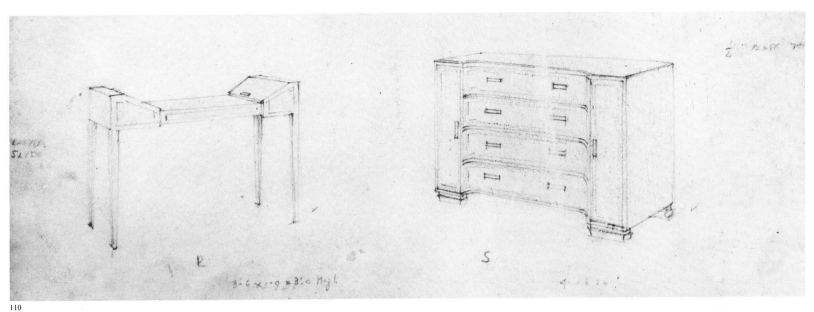

110

111

backs. Reminiscent of Hill's Baroque days was a wardrobe with scrolled pediment and bloated frieze. Much of his other furniture (he made more than sixty designs for the Thorntons) was in the 'moderne' style, in particular the bedroom furniture finished in apple green, cream or pink cracked lacquer with chintz hangings and upholstery, made by Heal & Son (figs. 110 & 111). Overall there is a wilful determination not to play the same game twice that distinguished Hill both as an architect and a designer.

Roderick Eustace Enthoven (*b.* 1900)

Designs for furniture for Mr and Mrs Graham Rawson, 5 Phillimore Terrace and 8 Campdėn Hill Square, London, 1932 and 1934.

112. Occasional table. Pencil with brown and yellow crayon on tracing paper (detail from sheet 315 x 625) *scale:* 1in to 1ft *h.* 2ft 4ins *w.* 1ft 7½ins *l.* 2ft 3ins.

113. Dining table. Pencil with brown and yellow crayon on tracing paper (355 x 285) *scale:* 1in to 1ft *h.* 2ft 4½ins *w.* 3ft *l.* 5ft 5ins.

For Charles Handley-Read[70] the Rawson household typified the discreetly forward looking taste of many upper class intellectuals in the 1930s. The Rawsons lived (from 1934) in a late Georgian terrace house of modest size, decorated in pale neutral colours and furnished with inherited pieces, a few bought antiques and some specially commissioned pieces. Also commissioned were two portraits by Rodrigo Moynihan and their collection of paintings and drawings included an Ivon Hitchens landscape. Theirs was 'a way of life anticipated from the beginning and consistently followed over many years, even a life time'.

For his sister Marion (Mrs Graham Rawson), Enthoven designed, after her marriage in 1930, at least a dozen pieces of furniture including a dining table and an occasional table. Both reveal his fondness for geometrically curved forms in furniture. Thus the three-decker occasional table (fig. 112) is elliptical while the dining table has convex ends to the top answered by the concavely curved uprights. Both were made in plywood veneered in a light toned wood and a medium toned macassar ebony. In the centre of the dining table is a flower container with concealed lighting adapted from a glass brick. Bell pushes are provided at each end to summon the maid and a bronze strip protects the plywood footrest.

Veneered plywood, cellulose sprayed, along with, for example, celluline (a superior kind of linoleum) were recently introduced materials in furniture construction. Enthoven used them for furniture of advanced design tempered by an innate classicism that, for instance, dictated that the upright to a standard lamp should be slightly entasised.

Enthoven designed a number of commissioned pieces in the 1930s, all made by Andrew Pegram Ltd of Camden Town. With perhaps two exceptions (the occasional table was repeated in a slightly smaller version once, a collapsible tea table was used three times) all were one-off pieces. Enthoven disliked repeating his designs and preferred to approach each commission afresh.

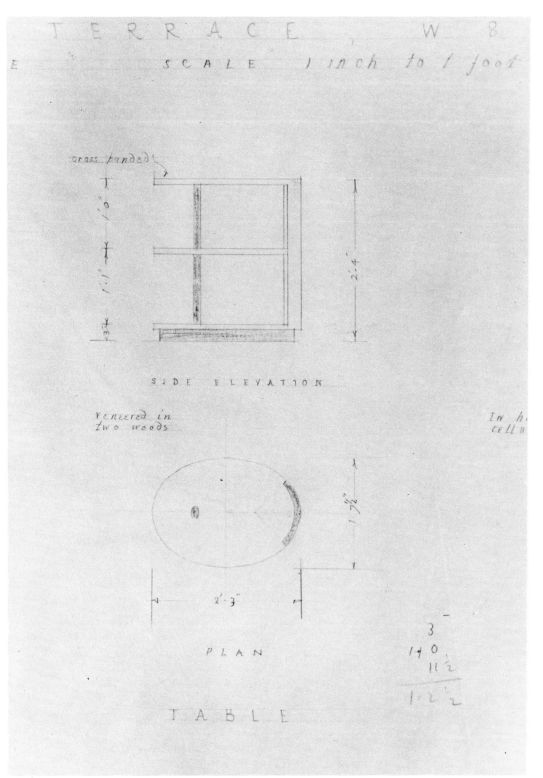

112

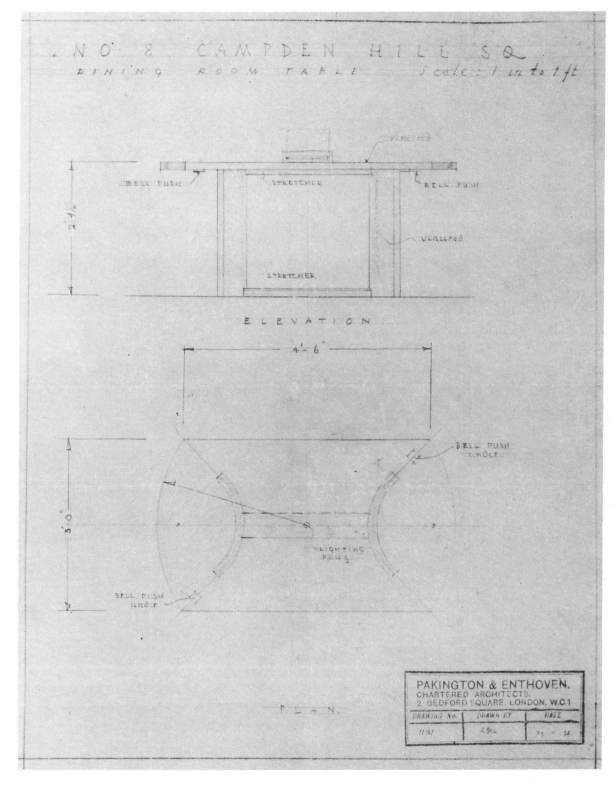

NO 8 CAMPDEN HILL SQ.
DINING ROOM TABLE   Scale : 1 in to 1 ft

ELEVATION

PLAN.

PAKINGTON & ENTHOVEN.
CHARTERED ARCHITECTS.
2 BEDFORD SQUARE, LONDON, W.C.1

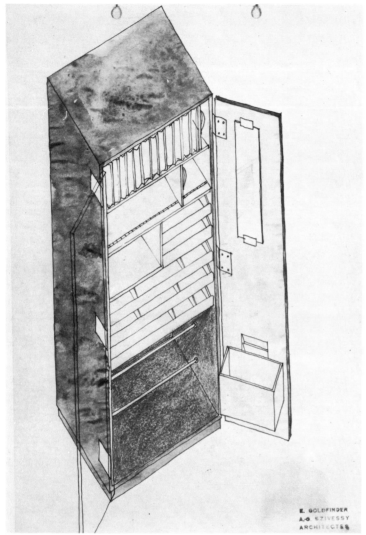

114

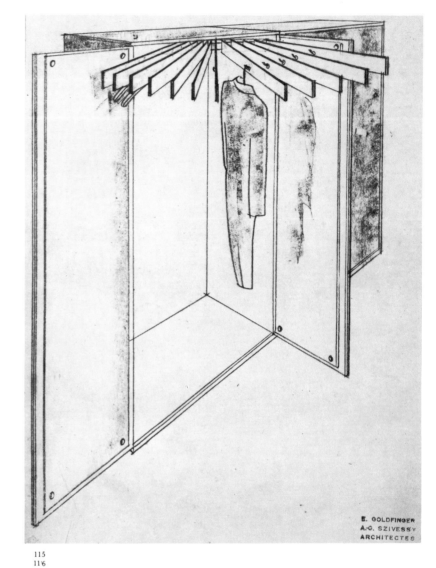

115
11'6

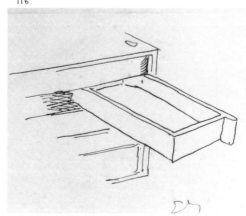

Ernö Goldfinger (*b.* 1902)

114. & 115. Designs for a clothes cupboard and wardrobe for Thonet Brothers, *c.* 1925. Pen and pencil with brown wash on tracing paper (300 x 215), pencil on tracing paper (265 x 210).

116. Design for pivoting drawers, *c.* 1928. Pen and pencil on tracing paper (310 x 230).

117. Design for a writing table, *c.* 1928. Pen on tracing paper (205 x 280).

118. Design for a child's safari chair, redrawn 1933. Pencil on tracing paper (730 x 1055) *scale*: full size *h.* 1ft 8¾ins *w.* 1ft 3ins *d.* 1ft 3⅛ins.

119. & 120. Designs for the living room and boys' bedroom for M and Mme Labousse, The Outlook, Cuq near Le Touquet, France, 1934. Prints with coloured washes and pencil added (310 x 380) *See* Plate XXII, p.118 (120).

121. Design for a stacking chair for Paul & Marjorie Abbatt Ltd, *c.* 1936. Pen on tracing paper (325 x 245) *h.* 1ft 7ins *w.* 1ft 3ins *d.* 1ft.

Born in Budapest, Goldfinger studied architecture in Paris during the 1920s and in 1934 moved his home and office to London. While he was studying at the Ecole des Beaux Arts he also (with Andre Szivessy until 1929) ran a practice designing showrooms, apartment interiors and furniture.

Many of Goldfinger's early designs for furniture exploited such new materials as tubular steel and bakelized paper. His design for pivoting drawers (fig. 116) relied on a metal casting as did the two pivoting drawers and a pivoting shelf of a writing table (fig. 117). A variant of this last was made in cellulosed wood for Richard Wyndham's studio flat in Paris in 1930.

Goldfinger explored, too, the potential of vernacular sources when he took the traditional Tunisian chair and used it as the basis of his design for a safari chair (fig. 118). His attachment to this type was shown in a series of re-designs over the next thirty years. The same use of off-beat sources was shown in his adaptation of ship's details to furniture design and his appropriation for domestic use of standard industrial fittings. Something of this piratical attitude appears in the furniture he designed for a holiday home near Le Touquet (figs. 119 & 120). In the bedroom for the two youngest boys were *matelot* bunk beds, pulleys, lashed canvas, a ladder and draughting lamps. The parents read in bed by the light of two *wagon-lit* bulkhead fittings. Safari chairs and a stool were used in the living room and dining chairs and beds were designed on similar lash-up principles.

Goldfinger designed toys and furniture for Paul & Marjorie Abbatt Ltd (from 1934) and also a shop in

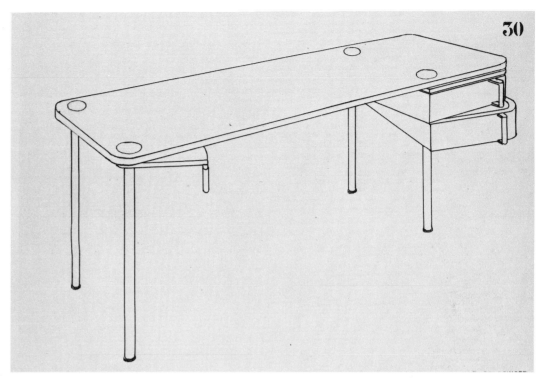

117

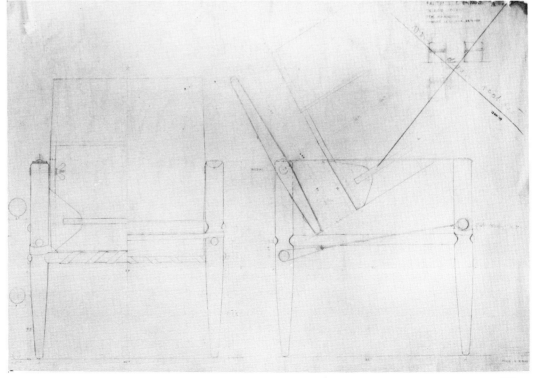

118

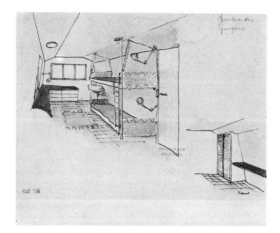

119

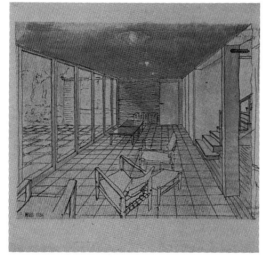

120

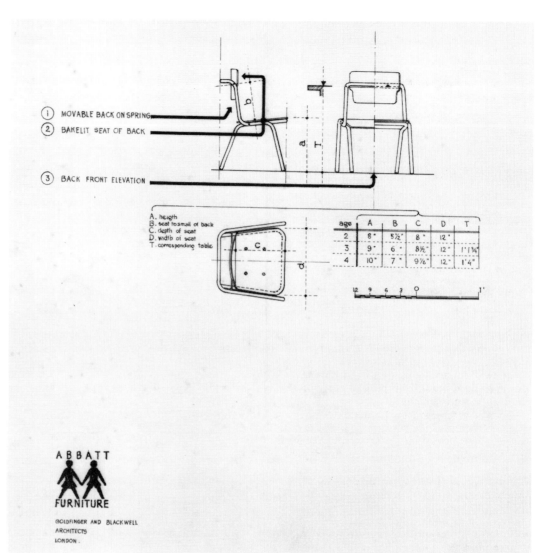

121

Wimpole Street, London (recently demolished). His designs for children reveal an unsuspected tenderness and two of his chairs, the safari chair and a stacking chair of chromed tubular steel and bakelized paper (later replaced by plywood) (fig. 121) were scaled down to childsize proportions. Goldfinger also designed units for Easiwork (from 1938) that were a development of an early concern with well organised and disciplined storage, as shown in a design for a clothes cupboard that included a shelf for filing away laundered shirts and a ventilated bin for discarded ones. And there was, as well, a matching wardrobe also designed for Thonet Brothers (figs. 114 & 115).

Marcel Breuer (1902-1981)

Designs for furniture for Mrs Dorothea Ventris, 47 Highpoint I, Highgate, London, 1936.

122. Easy chair. Pencil on tracing paper (370 x 410) *scale*: 1½ins to 1ft *h.* 3ft 6ins *w.* 3ft 8½ins *d.* 3ft 11ins.

123. Dining table. Pencil on tracing paper (detail from sheet 505 x 705) *scale*: 3ins to 1ft *h.* 2ft 4ins *w.* 2ft 7¼ins *l.* 5ft.

124. Writing table. Pencil on tracing paper (325 x 435) *scale*: 2ins to 1ft *h.* 2ft 5ins *w.* 4ft *d.* 2ft.

125. Dressing table. Pencil on tracing paper (490 x 720) *scale*: 1in to 1ft and full size Mirror *h.* 5ft 3ins *w.* 3ft 9ins, small chest of drawers *h.* 2ft 6ins *w.* 1ft 2ins *d.* 1ft 2ins, other storage units (overall) *h.* 2ft 6ins *w.* 8ft 4ins *d.* 1ft 2ins.

During his two years stay in London (1935-7) Breuer was in partnership with F.R.S. Yorke and was also design consultant to the Isokon Furniture Company. A commission to design the furniture and decoration of Mrs Dorothea Ventris's flat at Highpoint I (Lubetkin and Tecton, 1933-5) probably came through a mutual friend — Naum Gabo, the Constructivist sculptor. Flat 47 was a standard three-bedroomed apartment and the only modification Breuer made was to add a screen wall at one end of the living room.

The general scheme was fairly austere. In the living room, study and dining room, walls were painted white or lined with grass matting. The fitted carpet was white, the curtains were of undyed silk and the upholstery a dark reddish-brown. In the dining room a wall-hung, glass-fronted cabinet was stained black and so was the dining table. This had a blue bakelite top and the same material was used for the top of a freestanding electric fire. It was also used to line a hung cupboard with glass shelves in the living room. Here the furniture was of light toned birch or sycamore, veneered plywood or laminated wood. The rooms were lit by standard aluminium shop display reflectors and anglepoise lamps.

The disciplined use of white, grey, black, brown and blue accorded well with a Juan Gris painting and a Henry Moore grey carved stone figure on its Breuer-designed ebonized wood plinth. Breuer was against 'purely superficial "harmony" . . . realized by adopting either a formal or structural common denominator'. And his designs for furniture clearly demonstrate the principle that 'elements should receive different forms as a natural consequence of their different structure'.[71]

All of the furniture in Mrs Ventris's flat was designed by Breuer. Some were pieces in commercial production, some were developments of earlier ideas and some appear to be unadopted

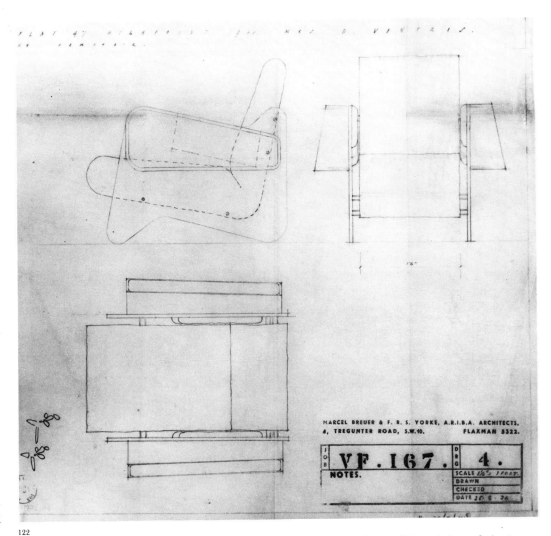

122

prototypes. The Isokon reclining chair and stacking tables were used and so was a cantilevered tubular steel, cane and ebonized wood chair (sometimes attributed to Mart Stam) designed in 1928 and manufactured by Thonet Brothers.

An entirely new and experimental design was that for an easy chair (fig. 122) with curved plywood sides and bent plywood arms that seems not to have been re-used. Another experimental piece was the dining table (fig. 123). Breuer had designed for Isokon stacking tables, each made from one piece of plywood bent in two places. The same idea used for larger tables failed and one reinforcement solution involving overlapping curved plywood planes is shown here.

Breuer had pioneered the use of chrome tubular steel for furniture during his years at the Bauhaus. For a desk for Michael Ventris (then aged fourteen)

Breuer designed one of his variations of a basic design with a glass table top supported on the left by a cabinet and supported on the right by a tubular steel U-frame (fig. 124). The glass top was attached to the frame by rubber rings only: friction held the two together.

A dressing table (fig. 125) designed for Mrs Ventris, in light toned sycamore with red bakelite tops, separates out the basic elements of drawers and mirrors. Here, the wall-fixed long mirror is attached to the wood-backed circular mirrors by piano hinges and the drawers are pivoted (an idea that Eileen Gray was exploiting in 1923). A cupboard with sliding doors and a wicker-fronted laundry box demonstrate Breuer's 'unit' approach to storage furniture.[72]

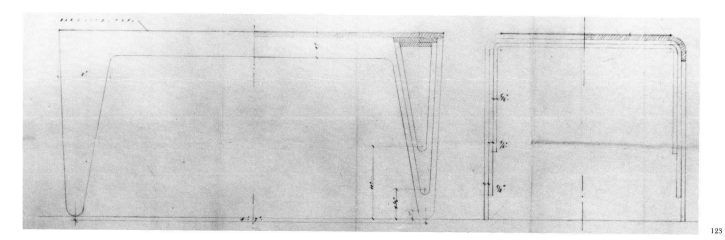

123

FLAT 47 HIGH POINT I·S MRS D. VENTRIS.
A WRITING DESK.

GLASS

MARCEL BREUER & F. R. S. YORKE, A.R.I.B.A: Architects,
4, TREGUNTER ROAD, S.W.10.   FLAXMAN 5822.

JOB		DRG	6.
NOTES.		SCALE	
VF.167.		DRAWN	
		CHECKED	
		DATE	

124

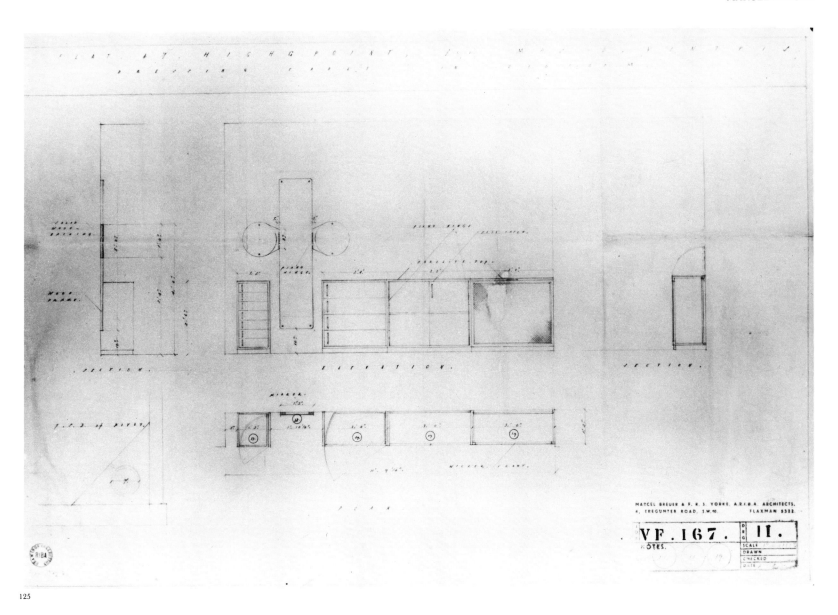

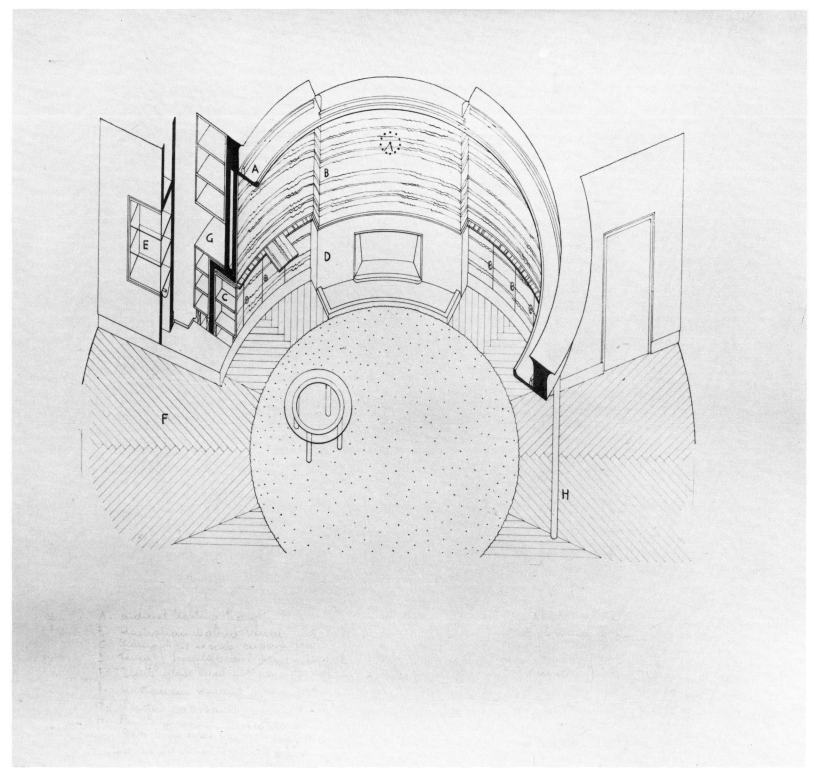

Raymond McGrath (1903-1977)

126. Design for the living room, St Ann's Hill, Chertsey, Surrey for C.R. Keene, *c.* 1936. Pen on tracing paper (510 x 625).

127. Design for a settee for the Vono Furniture Company, 1934. Pencil on tracing paper (540 x 450) *scale*: ½in to 1ft *h.* 2ft 9ins *w.* 8ft 6ins *d.* 2ft 6ins.

St Ann's Hill was McGrath's most ambitious piece of domestic architecture in England. Designed on a circular plan 'like a round of cheese with a slice cut out of it', it was built of reinforced concrete with three concentric ring beams supported on ten-inch columns on each floor.

The circle, or segments of it, was emphasised throughout the design. Christopher Tunnard's landscaping reflected it and so did the treatment of the interior. In the living room (fig. 126) this circular geometry was everywhere. A coved circular ceiling was answered by a circular rug, the fireplace wall was semicircular — its concave hearth matched on the opposite side of the room by a settee with a concave seat.[73] There were tub chairs and a circular table whose glass top was supported by a ring frame and cylindrical legs[74] — a paradigm of the structural system of the house.

McGrath was an advocate of fixed furniture that, where possible, was structurally part of the house. The living room wall at St Ann's Hill was made up of cupboards on two sides and with sliding shelves and a concealed lighting trough. Faced with Australian walnut veneer, the wall unit shows not only McGrath's predilection for strongly figured woods from his homeland but also his enthusiasm for new materials (terrazzo fireplace, black glass shelves) and for technical innovations (strip lighting). His approach to integral storage found its fulfilment in his designs for aeroplane interiors.

McGrath, who designed all the furniture for St Ann's Hill, also designed for at least three furniture making companies: Heal & Son, Easiwork and Vono. For Vono he designed a settee/bed (fig. 128) with a dressing table at one end and, most essential, a cocktail cabinet at the other. The functionalism of this piece was more apparent than real and it shares the flashiness of much of McGrath's earlier work.

127

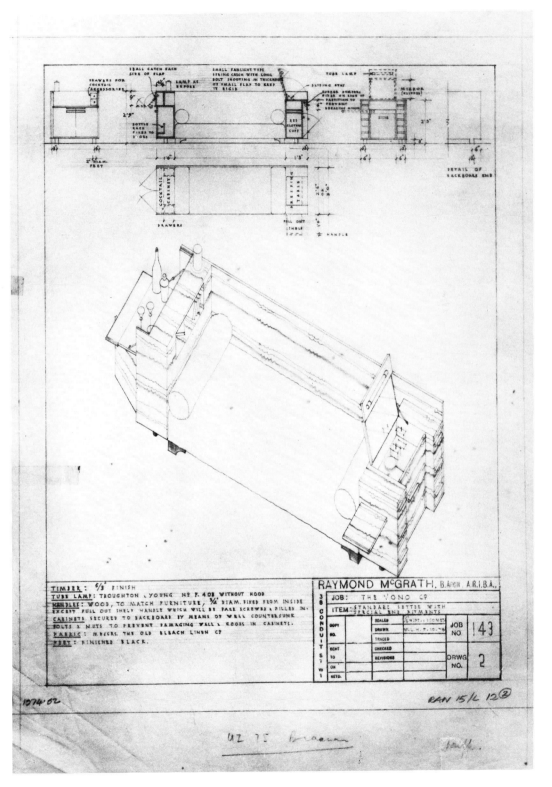

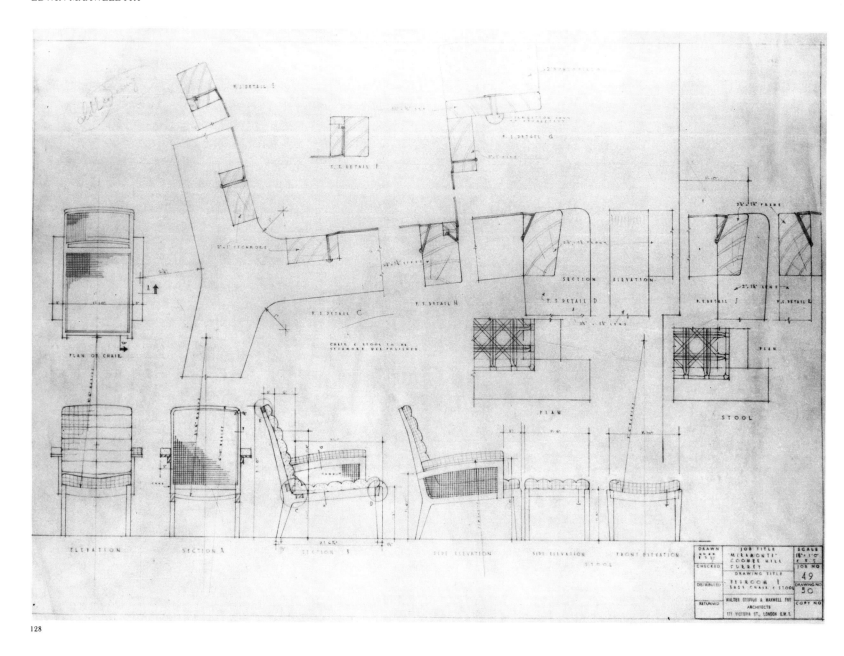

Edwin Maxwell Fry (*b.* 1899)

Designs for furniture for Jeremiah Green, Miramonte, Warren Rise, Kingston upon Thames, London, 1937.

128. Easy chair and stool. Pencil on tracing paper (540 x 750) *scale*: 1½ins to 1ft and full size Chair *h.* 3ft *w.* 2ft 4ins *d.* 2ft 11ins, stool *h.* 1ft 2ins *w.* 1ft 10ins *d.* 1ft 6ins.

129. Settee. Pencil on tracing paper (470 x 700) *scale*: 1in and 3ins to 1ft *h.* 2ft 9ins *w.* 11ft *d.* 2ft 8ins.

130. Axonometric of bedroom. Pencil with brown wash and pastels (440 x 565) *see* Plate XXI, p.117.

In his *Autobiographical Sketches* (1975) Fry wrote that 'Jerry Green . . . was the best client I ever had'. On a pleasant wooded site Fry designed for the bookmaker turned land speculator a house whose reinforced concrete construction, ribbon windows and flat roof conformed to the canons of International Modernism. Elements and details such as the garden terrace roof with framed views, the juxtaposition of rubble masonry with smooth concrete walls, cut-string concrete stair, the use of small diameter cylindrical columns and much else, underlined Fry's debt to Le Corbusier.

Though some furniture was bought (an Aalto armchair and occasional table, Breuer's reclining chair) most of it was designed in the architect's office (and in particularly by Jack Howe, chief assistant from 1936 to 1940) and made by B. Cohen & Son Ltd. Fry made considerable use of new materials or of materials newly used in furniture construction: latex foam, veneered blockboards and plywood, tubular steel as well as more traditional materials such as cane and leather used in new ways.

An easy chair and stool (fig. 128) was designed with a sycamore frame, the voids filled in with cane, overlain by cloth-covered dunlopillo. Writing tables and occasional tables veneered in walnut, rosewood or figured beech had slightly rounded corners and circular sectioned legs. Chromed tubular steel was used for a crescent-shaped settee (fig. 129) in two parts each with three runners and with vermillion leather upholstery. Fry's design for one of the guest bedrooms (fig. 130) shows how the ribbon window called for a new approach to room design. The solution lay in a minimum of furniture with wardrobe, chest of drawers, linen cupboard and dressing table forming a twinned partition between two bedrooms: the logical integration of furniture with architecture. The bed and tables were designed by Fry — not used however, were the bentwood chairs.

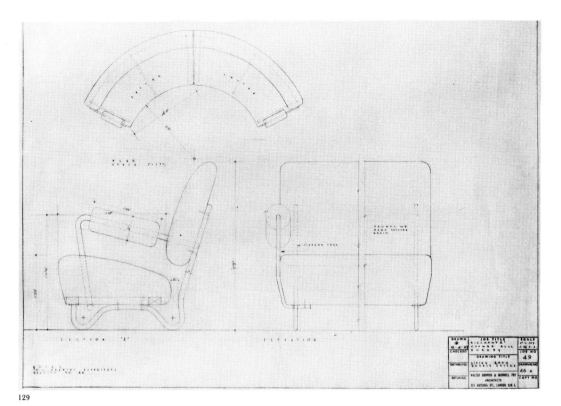

129

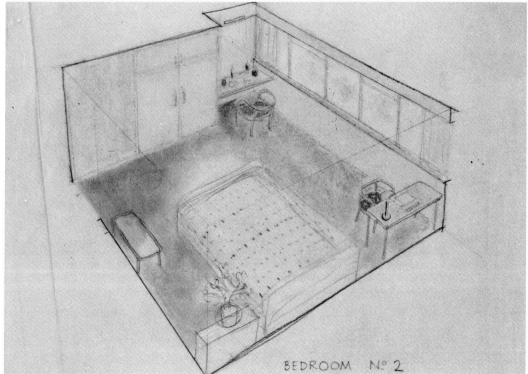

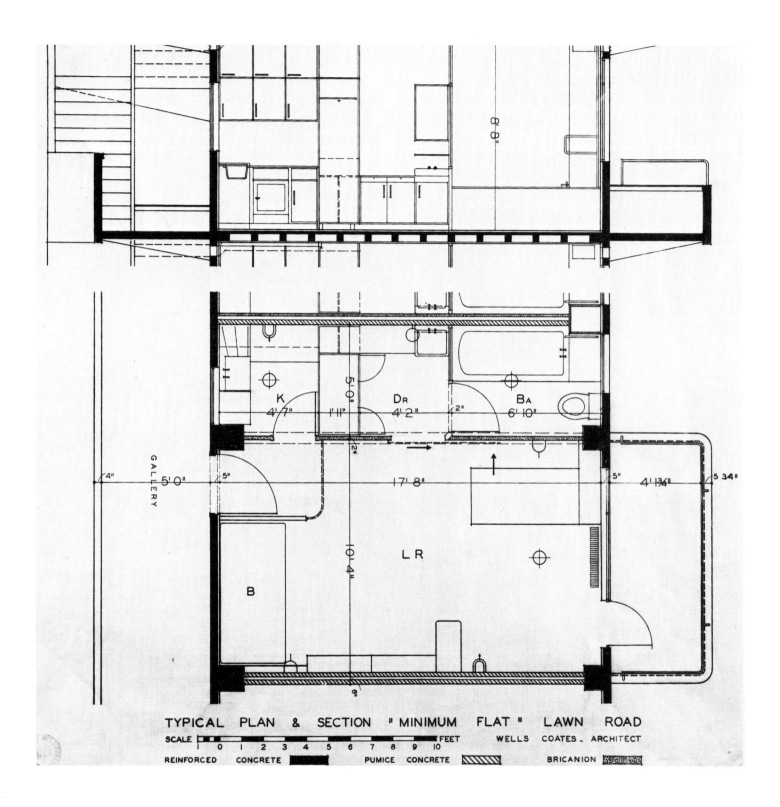

TYPICAL PLAN & SECTION "MINIMUM FLAT" LAWN ROAD

SCALE |‖‖‖‖‖|‖‖‖‖| 0 1 2 3 4 5 6 7 8 9 10 FEET   WELLS COATES _ ARCHITECT

REINFORCED   CONCRETE ▰   PUMICE CONCRETE ▨   BRICANION ▦

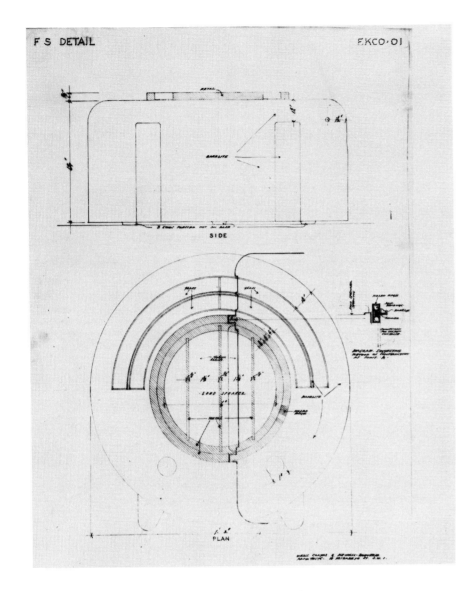

FS DETAIL   EKCO·OI

SIDE

PLAN

Wells Coates (1895-1958)

131. Design for a wireless case for E.K. Cole Ltd, 1934. Pencil on tracing paper (740 x 545) *scale*: full size *diam.* 1ft 2ins *d.* 6¾ins.

132. Design for a 'minimum flat', Lawn Road, Hampstead, London for Isokon Ltd, 1933-4. Pen on linen (450 x 425) *scale*: ½in to 1ft.

As well as specially commissioned pieces, Wells Coates designed furniture for Isokon, PEL and P.E. Gane that was 'simple in line, economical and sometimes elegant'.[75] All the same his greatest contributions to furniture design probably lie in his invention of the aluminium D-handle specifically designed for built-in furniture (1928), his

transformation of the wireless set from furniture into equipment and his 'minimum flat' that needed virtually no loose furniture.

Coates's design for the AD65 Ekco wireless set (fig. 131) was the result of a competition held in 1932, Coates won it with a circular design that exploited the possibilities of a new material — bakelite, and gave the radio a distinctive and logical form independent of cabinet-making techniques and traditions.

A built-in radio was part of Wells Coates's 'minimum flat' (fig 132). With a drinks cupboard and electric fire it formed one of three plywood unit fitments that also provided bookshelves, writing table and sideboard. A dining table mounted on a

sliding-rail and a built-in divan together with fitted kitchenette, dressing room and bathroom (in spaces 5 feet deep) meant that only dining chairs and an easy chair need be imported by the tenant. Twenty-two out of the twenty-nine flats at Lawn Road were 'minimal'.

Notes

1 *Read's Weekly Journal*, 15 July 1732, quoted in G. Beard, 'William Kent and the Royal Barge', *Burlington Magazine*, CXII, 1970, p.492

2 M. Jourdain, *The Work of William Kent*, 1948, p.82

3 A. Coleridge, 'John Vardy and the Hackworth Suite', *Connoisseur*, CXLIX, 1962, pp.12-17

4 Now preserved at Kedleston Hall

5 James Wyatt's design and working drawings for the drawing room, dining rom and staircase at Aldewarke Hall, 1775, are in the RIBA Drawings Collection

6 The designs shown here are not signed and are attributed to Porden on the evidence of draughtsmanship and of probability.

7 W. Papworth, 'Memoir of Joseph Bonomi, Architect and A.R.A.', *RIBA Transactions*, 1st series XIX, 1868-9, p.133

8 A.E. Richardson, 'The House', *Southill, a Regency House*, S. Whitbread (ed.), 1951, p.7

9 No extant examples of this type of furniture are known.

10 Essay on architecture with notes on, for example, 'The Caryatids' RIBA MSS Collection, SMK 2/20-21, ff.50-52

11 N. Whittock, The *Decorative Painters' and Glaziers' Guide*, 1827, p.91

12 The design shown here was re-used for at least one other client — Frederick Cass in 1833.

13 A.W.N. Pugin, MS autobiography, Library of the Victoria and Albert Museum, 86.MM.13

14 B. Ferrey, *Recollections of A.N. Welby Pugin and his Father, Augustus Pugin*, 1861, p.67

15 A.W.N. Pugin, *The True Principles of Pointed or Christian Architecture*, 1841, pp.34, 37

16 J. Harris, *Catalogue of British Drawings for Architecture . . . in American Collections*, 1971, pls 244-7 reproduce some of Wyatt's drawings for Lilleshall Hall

17 Obituary quoted in S. Trubshaw, *Family Records*, 1876, p.58

18 C.J. Richardson, *The Englishman's House*, 1870, p.339

19 According to the suggestion of Mr Geoffrey Fisher

20 *Photographs: own Furniture*, pp.22-23, in the RIBA Photographs Collection

21 W. Burges, *Art Applied to Industry*, [1865], p.76

22 E.W. Godwin, 'The House of an English Architect', *Art Journal*, new series, 1886, p.302

23 *Building News*, XXXVIII, 1880, p.497 (article on the Tower House, Melbury Road, London)

24 Mrs [H.R.] Haweis, *Beautiful Houses*, 1882, p.17

25 R.P. Pullan, 'The Late W. Burges and his Works' *Builder*, XLII, 1882, p.481

26 In the Library of the Victoria and Albert Museum, 86.SS.52

27 The 'walnut table with top to go up and down' was made for £10 by Mr Walden: Burges's estimate book (entry for 11 February 1876), Library of the Victoria and Albert Museum, 86.SS.52

28 In the RIBA Drawings Collection

29 W. Burges, 'Architectural Drawing', *RIBA Transactions*, 1st series, XI, 1860-1, pp.15-28

30 Quoted by C. Handley-Road, 'Aladdin's Palace in Kensington', *Country Life*, CXXXIX, 1966, p.600

31 W.R. Lethaby, *Philip Webb and his Work*, 1935, p.73

32 Dismantled in the 1950s but recently (1979) restored

33 *Building News*, XIV, 1867, p.222 (article on Castle Dromore)

34 C. Handley-Read, 'William Burges', *Victorian Architecture*, P. Ferriday (ed.), 1963, p.209

35 In the Prints and Drawings Department of the Victoria and Albert Museum, E230, E272, E274, E285, E287-1963

36 Burges used Turkish lattice work *(mushrabina)* for the window screens of his rooms in Buckingham Street: the drawings (in the RIBA Drawings Collection) for these are not dated but are of about 1862

37 Specifications of furniture dated *Dec.22 1869* and *Oct.7 1870* in the RIBA MSS Collection, G/DRO/3. A catalogue published by William Watt's Art Furniture Company (and available only in the British Library), *Art Furniture from Designs by E.W. Godwin and Others*, 1877, illustrates the circular settee (pl.12), the sofa with pierced ends (pl.15), 'light chairs with plaited fine straw backs' (pl.16, 'economic furniture') and the eagle chair (p.11, 'library chair'). The drawing room wall elevations are in the RIBA Drawings Collection, E.W. Godwin [17]-80 & 81

38 In the Prints and Drawings Department of the Victoria and Albert Museum E272-1963.

39 A. Warrington, 'Furniture at the Architectural Exhibition', *Builder*, XIX, 1861, p.290

40 According to the suggestion of Mr Clive Wainwright

41 In the RIBA Drawings Collection

42 *An Architectural and General Description of the Town Hall, Manchester*, W.E. Axon (ed.), 1878, p.2.

43 A survey of Waterhouse's furniture for Manchester Town Hall was begun in November 1980 under the supervision of Julian Treheurz and Deborah Clarke of the Manchester City Art Gallery, assisted by Sally MacDonald, and promises to produce some interesting results.

44 M.D. Conway, *Travels in South Kensington*, 1882, p.159

45 *Studio*, III, 1894, p.49 reproduces Albert Moore's designs for the four plaques

46 Philip Webb's account book, 1852-78, in the Library of the Victoria and Albert Museum, 35M 168

47 W.R. Lethaby, *Philip Webb and his Work*, 1935, p.106

48 G.G. Scott Junior, account book, 1867-91, RIBA MSS Collection, ScGGJ/24/1

49 In the possesion of Robert Hanbury Es. Extracts from which have very kindly been shown to me by Hilary Grainger whose doctrinal dissertation is on the work of George Peto.

50 *C.F.A. Voysey: Architect and Designer, 1857-1941*, 1978, introduction by J. Brandon-Jones, p.22

51 Manuscript of a lecture on interior decoration given to the Scottish Architectural Association by George Walton, 1898/9, in the RIBA MSS Collection

52 Photographs of Alma House, in the *Studio Yearbook*, 1907, pp.77, 97 suggest that a buffet to another design by

Walton was executed 1979, p.196, ed. D. Sharpe.

53 H. Muthesius, *The English House*.

54 As can be seen in a photograph of the library published in *Architectural Review*, XXI, 1907, p.171 (article on 8 Addison Road, Kensington)

55 *Arts and Crafts Exhibition Society Catalogue*, [1890], p.34

56 E. Wood, 'Colour-Decoration', *Building News*, CII, 1912, pp.117-118

57 Birkby Lodge exists still and is owned now by Hopkinson's Ltd. While, for example, the chimneypiece remains, the frieze painted on canvas has been removed and is now in the care of the John Rylands University Library, Manchester

58 Notes inscribed on another of Wood's designs for painted furniture, RIBA Drawings Collection

59 *House Beautiful*, XXVI, 1909, p.73 (article on Hill Top)

60 Office drawing numbers for furniture designs in the RIBA Drawings Collection go beyond 1,000

61 H.S. Goodhart-Rendel, obituary notice on A.B. Pite, *RIBA Journal*, XLII, 1934, p.277

62 H.S. Goodhart-Rendel, *English Architecture Since the Regency*, 1953, p.201

63 A. Bennett, H.V. Lanchester and A. Fenn, *The Art of E.A. Rickards*, 1920, p.46

64 *Architectural Review*, XXXVIII, 1915, p.81 (article on 129 Grosvenor Road)

65 E. Maufe, 'Furnishing and Decorating the House', *Architectural Association Journal*, XLII, 1931, p.157

66 The table, like other of Maufe's furniture, was made by Crossley & Brown of 1035 Finchley Road, London. It is now in a private collection.

67 *Country Life*, LXII, 1927, p.845 (article on 40 Devonshire Mansions)

68 Details and identification of Miss Laye's cocktail cabinet from the Oliver Hill correspondence in the RIBA MSS Collection, HiO/39/1

69 *Star*, 17 January 1938, newspaper cutting in an Oliver Hill scrapbook, vol.13 HiO/Box 92, in the RIBA MSS Collection

70 It was Charles Handley-Read who 're-discovered' R.E. Enthoven as a furniture designer and bought from Marion Rawson the dining table and occasional table, the designs for which are re-produced here, now in the Victoria and Albert Museum, AW 34.1979. Handley-Read's notes on Enthoven's furniture are in the RIBA MSS Collection

71 M. Breuer, 'Where Do We Stand?' *Architectural Review*, LXXVII, 1935, pp.133-6

72 The furniture (most of it) survives still at a house in Hampstead designed by Michael (1922-1956) and Lois Ventris, 1951-4, the drawings for which are in the RIBA Drawings Collection

73 As can be seen in a photograph of the living room published in *Architectural Review*, LXXXII, 1937, p.122 (article on St Ann's Hill)

74 As executed the table had three not four legs

75 S. Cantacuzino, *Wells Coates, a Monograph*, 1978, p.28

Bibliography

General background
H. Colvin, *A Biographical Dictionary of British Architects 1600-1840,* London, 1978

R. Edwards, *The Shorter Dictionary of English Furniture,* London, 1964

General: medieval
P. Eames, *Medieval Furniture: Furniture in England, France and the Netherlands from the Twelfth to the Fifteenth Century,* London, 1977

General: 17th century
P. Thornton, *Seventeenth-Century Interior Decoration in England, France & Holland,* New Haven and London, 1978

General: 18th century
J. Fowler and J. Cornforth, *English Decoration in the 18th Century*, London, 2nd ed., 1978

E. Harris, *The Furniture of Robert Adam*, London, 1963

P. Ward-Jackson, *English Furniture Designs of the Eighteenth Century*, London, 1959

General: 19th century
P. Agius, *British Furniture 1880-1915,* London, 1978

I. Anscombe and C. Gere, *Arts & Crafts in Britain and America,* London, 1978

E. Aslin, *19th Century English Furniture,* London, 1962

Fine Art Society, *Architect-Designers, Pugin to Mackintosh*, catalogue of an exhibition, London, 1981

P. Floud, 'Victorian Furniture', pp.17-29 *The Concise Encyclopaedia of Antiques*, London, 1957, L.G.G. Ramsey (ed.)

M. Girouard, *Sweetness and Light: the 'Queen Anne' Movement, 1860-1900,* Oxford, 1977. Chapter VI, 'Fitting out the House Beautiful'.

C. Handley-Read, 'The Nineteenth Century: England 1830-1901'; 'England 1901-1918', pp.207-231, *World Furniture*, 1965, H. Hayward (ed.)

S. Jervis, *Victorian Furniture,* London, 1968

E.T. Joy, *English Furniture, 1800-1851*, London, 1977

F. MacCarthy, *A History of British Design 1830-1970*, London, 1979

H. Muthesius, *The English House,* London, 1979, D. Sharp (ed.). Part III, 'The Interior'

R.W. Symonds and B.B. Whineray, *Victorian Furniture*, London, 1962

Victoria and Albert Museum, *Catalogue of an Exhibition of Victorian & Edwardian Decorative Arts,* London, 1952

Victorian and Edwardian Decorative Art: the Handley-Read Collection, catalogue of an exhibition, Royal Academy of Arts, London, 1972

S. Jervis, 'Cottage, Farm and Villa Furniture, *Burlington Magazine* CXVII, 1975 pp.848-59

N. Pevsner 'Art Furniture of the Eighteen-Seventies', *Architectural Review*, CXI 1952, pp.43-50

General: twentieth century
M. Battersby, *The Decorative Twenties,* New York, 1969

M. Battersby, *The Decorative Thirties,* London, 1971

N. Carrington, *Design in the Home,* London, 1933. Revised edition, *Design and Decoration in the Home*, London, 1938

E. Goldfinger, *British Furniture Today*, London, 1951

J.L. Martin and S. Speight, *The Flat Book,* London and Hertford, 1939

Modern Chairs 1918-1970, catalogue of an exhibition, Whitechapel Art Gallery, London, 1970

J.C. Rogers, *Modern English Furniture,* London, 1930

Individual architects
John Talman: T. Friedman, 'The English Appreciation of Italian Decoration', *Burlington Magazine*, CXVII, 1975, pp.841-7

William Kent: P. Norton, *State Barges*, National Maritime Museum, Greenwich, 1972, pp.15-21
G. Beard, 'William Kent and the Royal Barge', *Burlington Magazine*, CXII, 1970, pp.488-95
A.E. Richardson, 'The Royal Barge', *RIBA Journal*, XXXVIII, 3rd series, 1931, pp.172-6

John Vardy: A. Coleridge, 'John Vardy and the Hackwood Suite', *Connoisseur,* CXLIX, 1962, pp.12-17

James Stuart: N. Goodison, 'Mr Stuart's Tripod', *Burlington Magazine,* CXIV, 1972, pp.695-705
J. Hardy and H. Hayward, 'Kedleston Hall, Derbyshire', *Country Life,* CLXIII, 1978, pp.194-7; 262-6
J. Harris, 'Newly Acquired Designs by James Stuart in the British Architectural Library Drawings Collection', *Architectural History,* XXII, 1979, pp.74-7, pl. 16-27

J.B. Papworth: G. McHardy, *Office of J.B. Papworth, Catalogue of the Drawings Collection of the Royal Institute of British Architects,* Farnborough, 1977
E.T. Joy, 'A Versatile Victorian Designer: J.B. Papworth', *Country Life,* CXLVII, 1970, pp.130-1

Sir Charles Barry and the Reform Club: J. Mordaunt Crook, *The Reform Club,* London, 1973
London Interiors [1841], I, pp.145-52
The Architect, II, 1869, pp.201-2
Building News, XXXV, 1878, p.551

A.W.N. Pugin: Victoria and Albert Museum, *Furniture in the House of Lords,* London, 1974
A. Wedgwood, *The Pugin Family, Catalogue of the Drawings Collection of the Royal Institute of British Architects,* Farnborough, 1977
C. Wainwright, 'A.W.N. Pugin's Early Furniture', *Connoisseur,* CXCI, 1976, pp.32-43

William Burges: R.P. Pullan, *The House of William Burges, A.R.A.,* London, 1885
E.W. Godwin, 'The Home of an English Architect', *Art Journal,* 1886, new series, pp.170-3; 301-5
C. Handley-Read, 'Notes on William Burges's Painted Furniture', *Burlington Magazine,* CV, 1963, pp.496-509
C. Handley-Read, 'Aladdin's Palace in Kensington', *Country Life,* CXXXIX, 1966 pp.600-604

E.W. Godwin: E. Aslin, *The Furniture Designs of E.W. Godwin,* Victoria and Albert Museum Bulletin Reprints 13, London, 1970

George Aitchison: M. Richardson, *George Aitchison, Lord Leighton's Architect,* catalogue of an exhibition, RIBA Heinz Gallery, London, 1980

Philip Webb: N. Cromey-Hawke, 'William Morris and Victorian Painted Furniture', *Connoisseur,* CXCI, 1976, pp.32-43

C.F.A. Voysey: J. Brandon-Jones and others, *C.F.A. Voysey: Architect and Designer 1857-1941,* catalogue of an exhibition, Brighton Art Gallery and Museum, London, 1978
D. Simpson, *C.F.A. Voysey, an Architect of Individuality,* London, 1979

J. Symonds, *C.F.A. Voysey, Catalogue of the Drawings Collection of the Royal Institute of British Architects,* Farnborough, 1976

George Walton: T. Howarth, *C.R. Mackintosh,* 1952, pp.233-8
G. and C. Larner, *The Glasgow Style,* London, 1980, pp.3-5
N. Pevsner, 'George Walton', *RIBA Journal,* XLVI, 3rd series, 1939, pp.176-188

Edgar Wood: J. Archer and S. Evans, *Partnership in Style: Edgar Wood & J. Henry Sellers,* catalogue of an exhibition, Manchester City Art Gallery, 1975
J. Seddon, 'The Furniture Design of Edgar Wood', *Burlington Magazine,* CXVII, 1975, pp.589-67

Barry Parker: R.B. Parker and R. Unwin, *The Art of Building a Home,* London, 1901
Barry Parker & Raymond Unwin, architects, catalogue of an exhibition, Architectural Association, London, 1980
E.W. Gregory, 'The Dwelling-House of an Apostle of Health', *House Beautiful,* XXVI, 1909, pp.73-6

Sir Edwin Lutyens: *Lutyens: the Work of the English Architect Sir Edwin Lutyens (1869-1944),* catalogue of an exhibition, Hayward Gallery, London, 1981

Sir Giles Gilbert Scott: 'No. 129 Grosvenor Road, London, S.W.' *Architectural Review,* XXXVIII, 1915, pp.80-1

Oliver Hill: C. Reilly, 'A Devonshire House flat', *Country Life,* LXII, 1927, pp.845-9

Ernö Goldfinger: J. Lowrie, 'The Work of Ernö Goldfinger', *Architectural Design,* XXXIII, 1963, pp.9-54

Marcel Breuer: C. Buckley, **Isokon,** catalogue of an exhibition, Hatton Gallery, University of Newcastle upon Tyne, 1980
Furniture by Godwin and Breuer, Catalogue of an exhibition, Bristol Art Gallery, 1976
C. Wilk, *Marcel Breuer: Furniture and Interiors,* New York, 1981
'Flat at Highpoint, Highgate', *Architectural Review,* LXXXI, 1937, pp.192-4

Raymond McGrath: 'St Ann's Hill, Chertsey, Surrey', *Architectural Review,* LXXXII, 1937, p.117-122

E. Maxwell: 'A Surrey House in a Park', *Architectural Review,* LXXXII, 1937, pp.187-92

Wells Coates: C. Buckley, *Isokon,* catalogue of an exhibition, Hatton Gallery, University of Newcastle upon Tyne, 1980
S. Cantacuzino, *Wells Coates, a monograph,* London and Bedford, 1978

Subject Index to illustrations

The pages on which subjects are illustrated are given in italics.
Roman numerals refer to the colour plates.

Index of Names

The pages on which subjects are illustrated are given in italics.
Roman numerals refer to the colour plates.